VICTORIA = Albert of Saxe - Coburg - Gotha
(b. 1819)   Prince Consort
1837-1901   1819-61

exandra   = EDWARD VII (2)   Alfred   Helena   Louise   Arthur   Leopold   Beatrice
Denmark   b 1841   Duke of   Princess   Duchess   Duke of   Duke of   Princess
44-1925   1901-10   Edinburgh   Christian   of Argyll   Connaught   Albany   Henry of
                              1844-1900   of Schleswig-   1848-1939   1850-1942   1853-84   Battenberg
                                             Holstein   1858-1944
                                             1846-1923

GEORGE V = Mary of Teck   Louise   = Alexander Duff   Victoria   Maud   = Haakon VII
e b 1865   1867-1953   Princess Royal   Duke of Fife   1868-1935   1869-1938   of Norway
1910-36   1867-1931   1849-1912   1872-1957

= Elizabeth   Mary   = Henry   Henry   = Alice Montagu-   George   = Marina   John
Bowes-Lyon   Princess Royal   Viscount Lascelles Duke of   Douglas-Scott   Duke of Kent   Princess of   1905-19
b. 1900   1897-1965   6th Earl of Harewood Gloucester   b. 1901   1902-42   Greece
                                 1882-1947   1900-74   1906-68

ld   = Angela   William   Richard   = Birgitte   Edward   = Katharine   Alexandra = Angus Ogilvy   Michael = Marie-Christine
elles Dowding   1941-72   Duke of   van Deurs   Duke of   Worsley   b. 1936   b. 1928   b. 1942   von Reibnitz
24   b. 1919   Gloucester   b. 1946   Kent   b. 1933   b. 1945
                                b. 1944   b. 1935

    Henry   Alexander   Davina   Rose   George   = Sylvana   Helen   Nicholas   James = Julie   Marina   = Paul
    b. 1953   Earl of   b. 1977   b. 1980   Earl of   Tomaselli   b. 1964   b. 1970   b. 1964 Rawlinson   b. 1966   Mowatt
                Ulster   St Andrews   b. 1957   b. 1964
                b. 1974   b. 1962

ry   Amy   Edward   Frederick   Gabriella
       b. 1986   Lord Downpatrick   b. 1979   b. 1982
                                                 b. 1988

A Princely Marriage

Also by Anthony Holden

BIOGRAPHY

The St Albans Poisoner
Charles, Prince of Wales
Their Royal Highnesses
The Queen Mother
Olivier
Charles (new edition)
Big Deal

JOURNALISM

Of Presidents, Prime Ministers and Princes
The Last Paragraph (ed.)

TRANSLATION

Aeschylus's *Agamemnon*
Greek Pastoral Poetry
Mozart's *Don Giovanni*

A Princely Marriage

CHARLES & DIANA • THE FIRST TEN YEARS

Text by Anthony Holden
Photographs by Kent Gavin

BANTAM PRESS

LONDON · NEW YORK · TORONTO · SYDNEY · AUCKLAND

TRANSWORLD PUBLISHERS LTD
61–63 Uxbridge Road, London W5 5SA

TRANSWORLD PUBLISHERS (AUSTRALIA) PTY LTD
15–23 Helles Avenue, Moorebank, NSW 2170

TRANSWORLD PUBLISHERS (NZ) LTD
Cnr Moselle and Waipareira Aves, Henderson, Auckland

Published 1991 by Bantam Press
a division of Transworld Publishers Ltd
Copyright © Anthony Holden and Kent Gavin 1991

The right of Anthony Holden and Kent Gavin to be identified
as authors of this work has been asserted in accordance
with sections 77 and 78 of the Copyright Designs and
Patents Act 1988.

British Library Cataloguing in Publication data

Holden, Anthony *1947*
A princely marriage
1. Great Britain. Charles, Prince of Wales, 1948.
Diana, Princess of Wales
I. Title
941.085092

ISBN 0-593-02350-1

Designed by Bob Searles of Associated Design Consultants Ltd, London
Typeset in Garamond Simoncini by Andy Clements of Lazy Dog, London
Printed in Great Britain by Butler & Tanner Ltd, Frome and London

*'A princely marriage is the brilliant
edition of a universal fact,
and as such it rivets mankind'*

– Walter Bagehot, *The English Constitution*

CONTENTS

INTRODUCTION

I
WORLDS APART

II
A PUBLIC ROMANCE

III
MIDSUMMER TRUMPETS

IV
THE TENTATIVE PRINCESS

V
'AN HEIR AND A SPARE'

VI
AT HOME

VII
FLYING THE FLAG

VIII
THE TRANSFORMATION OF A PRINCESS

IX
THE TRANSFORMATION OF A PRINCE

X
TOWARDS 2000: THE NEXT TEN YEARS

INTRODUCTION

*When Charles, Prince of Wales, married Lady Diana Spencer in July 1981,
the heady mixture of ceremonial, sunshine and street parties brought
much-needed relief to an otherwise difficult summer for Britain. Even the
spectre of civil disruption around the land, with ugly riots from Brixton to
Toxteth, did little to ruffle the fairy-tale aura bedecking the bride, a strikingly
beautiful innocent of barely twenty, the first English girl to marry an heir to the
throne in more than 300 years. Half the nation, it seemed, fell for her quite as
unconditionally as her prince.*

*Ten years on, it is hard to remember how the royal family ever managed
without Diana, Princess of Wales. With her youth, her openness, her photogenic
charms, she has single-handedly rejuvenated not just her husband, but an
institution which, if in no imminent danger of collapse, had become perhaps a
little frayed at the edges. Thanks in large part to Diana, the British Crown
approaches the twenty-first century as popular as at any time in its history.*

*This is the story of that remarkable decade – above all the story of a shy
young girl who has matured into an accomplished and elegant Queen-in-waiting,
at the same time enabling her husband to grow from a frustrated, somewhat
tortured soul into a self-confident, substantial force in the contemporary world.
It is about the art of becoming royal as much as the art of being royal;
of smiling one's way through the ups and downs of any marriage; and of
raising children destined, perhaps, to play an even bigger role in the history of
a new millennium.*

I

WORLDS
APART

—— · ——

July 1st, 1969 was an unhappy eighth birthday for a shy Norfolk prep school girl, enduring the knowing looks of her fellow pupils as the national newspapers revelled in her parents' high society divorce case. Lady Diana Spencer spent the day, like the rest of the nation, huddled around a television, watching the BBC's first major outside broadcast in colour: live from Caernarvon Castle, the investiture of Charles Philip Arthur George, twenty-year-old heir apparent to the British throne, as Prince of Wales.

DIANA HAD ONCE met the Prince, though she could scarcely be expected to remember it. The twelve-year-old schoolboy had come round to congratulate her parents, close friends of his own, when their third daughter had been born on the Sandringham estate eight years before. He was a Cheam schoolboy, on the verge of public school, his life lived in the public spotlight since the moment it was announced that his mother was pregnant; she was born to a noble family on the edge of the royal circle. But their childhoods could scarcely have been more different – his at the heart of the nation's most famous nuclear family, hers amid the unhappy maelstrom of a broken home.

ALMOST TWENTY years after that first meeting, after a decade and more of pressure to find himself a bride, Prince Charles finally fell for the girl, quite literally, next door. Diana Frances Spencer was born on 1 July 1961, at Park House on the Sandringham estate, which her father was then renting from the Queen. The new arrival was the third daughter of Edward John, Viscount Althorp, heir to the 7th Earl Spencer, and his wife Frances Ruth Burke Roche, daughter of the 4th Baron Fermoy. The Spencers were familiar figures at court: Diana's father had been the Queen's equerry on her Coronation tour of Australia in 1954, and her grandmother was one of the Queen Mother's few intimates. Like any good landlord, the Prince of Wales popped round to greet the proud parents with a bottle of champagne.

THOUGH IT WOULD END IN DIVORCE, THE SPENCER WEDDING WAS ONE OF THE SOCIETY EVENTS OF 1954. DIANA (RIGHT) WAS THE SPENCERS' THIRD DAUGHTER; THEY HAD BEEN HOPING FOR A SON.

THE HULTON-DEUTSCH COLLECTION

DIANA'S FATHER, if truth be told, was rather disappointed. Johnny Spencer had been hoping for a son and heir; he had seen one son die in infancy, and desperately wanted another to ensure the survival of his family's 200-year-old title. It would be three more years before his hopes were fulfilled in the shape of a younger brother for Diana – whom the Spencers would name Charles, after the Prince of Wales.

UNLIKE HER FUTURE husband's, however, Diana's happy home life would scarcely outlive her infancy. Even before the birth of her younger brother, her parents' marriage had begun to go awry. She was only six, and her brother Charles just three, when one day their mother Frances suddenly disappeared. That morning in 1967, as a family servant put it, Lady Althorp 'just wasn't there any more'. Diana's older sisters Sarah and Jane were twelve and ten, and their mother herself only thirty-three when she decided to put an end to her thirteen-year marriage to Johnny Spencer. The match had started in a blaze of glory; in 1954 Frances had been the youngest bride this century to have married in Westminster Abbey, with the new young Queen and her husband among the guests. But it had since then gone steadily downhill, reaching an acrimonious low point soon after Charles's birth in 1964. So weary was she of life with Johnny Spencer, whom she subsequently sued for divorce on the grounds of cruelty, that Frances was prepared to surrender not only her title, but her children, to escape from it. The split took Diana and her siblings totally by surprise.

THEIR PARENTS' divorce case was about as painful as it could be. Like the rest of the nation, eight-year-old Diana, now at a Norfolk boarding school, watched via the newspapers as her father mobilized sufficient character witnesses from the British aristocracy to make her mother's cruelty suit hopeless. She was forced to let him counter-sue her for adultery with Peter Shand-Kydd, a wallpaper millionaire, and she lost custody of her children in the process. The experience was so painful that to this day she will not speak of it.

THAT SAME year, hard upon her defeat in the courts, the former Viscountess Althorp became Mrs Shand-Kydd and transplanted herself to a new life in the remote north-west of Scotland. Now Diana and her siblings spent school holidays shuttling between Norfolk and Oban, where her mother settled into a happy new domesticity. As her father, meanwhile, grew morose in his unwonted bachelorhood, so Diana grew ever closer to her mother, who through many subsequent vicissitudes (including an eventual split with Shand-Kydd) has remained the dominant influence in her life.

DIANA WAS fourteen when, in 1975, her father became the 8th Earl Spencer on the death of his own father, Jack; her eleven-year-old brother Charles now became Viscount Althorp. So the family moved into the ancestral Spencer seat at Althorp (pronounced 'Altrup') in Northamptonshire, a 450-year-old, 1,500-acre stately home which boasted a fine collection of old masters, but also conferred on the new Earl the less welcome legacy of crippling death duties. Less than a year later, in the midst of dire financial difficulties, Johnny Spencer remarried – another divorcee, and a somewhat exotic one in the shape of Raine, Countess of Dartmouth, much-loved by gossip columnists as an outspoken London politician and daughter of the prolific romantic novelist Barbara Cartland.

RAINE DARTMOUTH'S arrival on the scene caused some dismay among the Spencer children. Her flamboyant style grated on them at first, and the sleepy halls of Althorp were not accustomed to her brand of new-broom dynamism. Raine was soon applying her celebrated energies to sprucing the place up, and generating new sources of income. It was a much-needed rejuvenation programme, but one which at times offended both family and local sensibilities, as she dismissed some long-standing members of staff, opened the house to the paying public and herself manned a gift shop for visitors in the stable block.

THE HULTON-DEUTSCH COLLECTION

But the Spencer children were reassured by the evident care and affection she lavished on their father, and were totally won over by the single-minded devotion with which she nursed him back to health after a near-fatal stroke in 1978 – just a week after a party celebrating Althorp's return to solvency.

B Y N O W transplanted to another boarding school in Kent, Diana was regarded as a 'thoroughly average' pupil – 'a perfectly ordinary, nice little girl who was always kind and cheerful'. Though she still saw the younger royals in the school holidays, she was beginning to make lasting friendships of her own, including the two girls who would later enjoy fleeting fame as her Chelsea flatmates. One term, there was a little gentle teasing as she exchanged letters with Prince Andrew, of whom she hung a photo over her bed. He was just a year older than her. One day, giggled her friends, there might even be a royal romance.

T H E R U M O U R S pursued Diana when she left school at sixteen, without any 'O' levels, to travel the well-worn path of well-born girls to finishing school in Switzerland. One of the few unorthodox moments in her early life soon followed, when she abruptly left after only six weeks, pleading homesickness. The most she brought home

FOUR-YEAR-OLD PRINCE CHARLES WAS CONSPICUOUSLY BORED BY HIS MOTHER'S CORONATION IN 1953, EIGHT YEARS BEFORE DIANA'S BIRTH.

with her from Montreux was a smattering of French, and some early experience on the nursery ski slopes.

HER FATHER agreed to set her up in a flat in London, where she was determined to find some sort of job and begin an independent life of her own. It was during these few months of nervous transition, with Diana on the threshold of adulthood, that she found herself standing in a ploughed field on a stretch of the Althorp estate called Nobottle Wood, handing round drinks to members of a visiting shoot. Among the guests was the Prince of Wales, then squiring her elder sister, Sarah. Diana, she has since confessed, thought him 'pretty amazing'. The future king, for his part, noticed for the first time how Sarah's younger sister had blossomed into a 'very amusing, and jolly, and attractive' sixteen-year-old.

ONLY ONCE, since visiting the youngest Spencer daughter in her cradle, had Charles made any significant gesture in her direction. In the summer of 1969, after his investiture at Caernarvon, the Prince had relaxed at Balmoral by writing a children's story for his brothers Andrew and Edward, then nine and five. Entitled *The Old Man of Lochnagar*, it was eventually to be published, in 1980, with drawings by his old friend Sir Hugh Casson. At the time, on returning to Sandringham, Charles ran off an extra copy for the little girl next door who sometimes played with his brothers.

BRITAIN'S FUTURE KING, heir to the throne since the age of three, had learnt to come to terms with his unenviable fate even before Diana was born. On the death of his grandfather, King George VI, in 1952, Prince Charles of Edinburgh was suddenly Duke of Cornwall and heir apparent. His mother, who had been hoping for many more years of relatively private family life before inheriting the

PRESS ASSOCIATION

DIANA (REAR, RIGHT) WAS A BRIDESMAID AT THE 1978 WEDDING OF HER SISTER JANE TO SIR ROBERT FELLOWES, NOW THE QUEEN'S PRIVATE SECRETARY.

JOHN TOPHAM PICTURE LIBRARY

throne, was suddenly busy all day – in a role for which she was so unprepared as often, in those early days, to be reduced to tears. The most she could do was persuade the then Prime Minister, Winston Churchill, to put back the hour of his weekly audience so that she could be with her children at bedtime.

L I K E   A   R E C E N T Prince of Wales – Queen Victoria's son, Bertie – Charles faced the prospect of waiting more than half a century to inherit the throne. Unlike Bertie, however, he had sympathetic and understanding parents, well aware of the difficulties of so long an apprenticeship, and prepared to learn from the mistakes of their forebears. The new Elizabethan era, so warmly hailed by Churchill, was one of cosy domestic monarchy, the First Family giving its people unprecedented glimpses into its private life by way of authorized books and television films. Prince Charles became the first heir apparent in British history to go to school with other children – albeit private schools for sons of the privileged – rather than being educated privately, behind palace walls. In time, showing an increasing penchant for setting precedents, he would become the first British heir to the throne to win himself a university degree.

H E   H A D   T H E advantage of a father with a normal, if disrupted, education, and a mother who knew that her own, at the hands of tutors, had been woefully inadequate. Prince Philip being head of the family in matters domestic, it was no coincidence that the schools eventually chosen for Charles were those attended by his father before him (his mother has admitted that she would have preferred Eton, closer to home at Windsor). After a brief stint as a day boy at Hill House School in London, mightily disrupted by the attentions of the press, he was despatched as a boarder to Cheam in Hampshire, and thence further afield to the remote northern wilds of Scotland, and Gordonstoun.

IN 1966 CHARLES LEFT GORDONSTOUN FOR TWO TERMS IN AUSTRALIA. SAID HIS PRIVATE SECRETARY, SIR DAVID CHECKETTS (REAR): 'I WENT OUT WITH A BOY AND CAME BACK WITH A MAN.'

CHARLES'S SCHOOLDAYS were far from happy, but he came in retrospect to decide that they were worthwhile. The heir to the throne was at a decided disadvantage in the brutal, amoral world of the British public schoolboy, however much good it may have done him to polish his own shoes, make his own bed and take his turn to empty the dustbins – as if, as the society columnists kept simpering, he were a 'normal' child. His two terms away from Gordonstoun, on an exchange at Geeling grammar school in Australia, were by far the happiest, least disrupted and most formative of his youth. 'I went out to Australia with a boy,' said his private secretary, David Checketts, 'and I came back with a man.'

AS HE GREW UP, the Prince was taught to understand, but not to abuse, his rank. If he left a door open, his father told palace footmen that he must learn to shut it for himself. If rude to servants, he was spanked and told to apologize; if he threw snowballs at them, they were instructed to forget protocol and throw some back. Once, at Sandringham, he was sent back out into the grounds to find a dog lead he had lost. 'Dog leads,' the Queen told her son, 'cost money.'

IN A SECULAR age, Elizabeth II attached a new importance to the monarchy's role as an exemplar of Christian family life. Intent on inching the institution closer to its people, while carefully preserving the essential gulf between the two, she made certain innovations more revolutionary than perhaps they seemed. She became the first British monarch, for instance, to abolish the custom whereby her children bow or curtsey in her presence. At Cambridge her son lived in his college, Trinity, whereas his grandfather, great-uncle and great-grandfather before him had lived in splendid isolation on the city outskirts, their tutors travelling to them, and their fellow students standing up whenever

DIANA WAS GROWING UP ON THE FRINGES OF THE ROYAL FAMILY AS CHARLES WAS INVESTED PRINCE OF WALES AT CAERNARVON (RIGHT) IN 1969.

SYNDICATION INTERNATIONAL

they entered the room. Neither George VI, Edward VII nor Edward VIII had risked taking a final exam; Charles did, and won himself a reassuringly average second-class degree.

RELUCTANTLY, AND against the wishes of his Cambridge tutors, he again took two terms out from his normal course of education – this time to attend the University College of Wales, Aberystwyth, as a gesture to his uncertain subjects in the principality of Wales. The date of his investiture at Caernarvon Castle – symbol, to the Welsh, of the English usurpation of their sovereignty – was drawing near. Charles thus became the first English Prince of Wales in the 700-year history of his office to take the trouble to learn to speak a few words of Welsh. Many of his predecessors had never even bothered to go near the place.

THE INVESTITURE was billed as the climax of his preparation for entry into public life, the moment for Charles to carve himself a lasting niche in the public consciousness. It was the culmination of a carefully calculated two-year plan for the marketing of a Prince of Wales, devised by Checketts, a former public relations man, at the Queen's behest. But the timing proved to be unfortunate: it was the last year of the first Wilson government, a period of public austerity, which coincided with the rise of a fierce strain of nationalism around the principality. With terrorist bombs going off all over Wales, threats being made on the Prince's life, and the Government vetoing all suggestions that the ceremony be called off, the

lavish mini-coronation of the Prince of Wales looked like being the first serious mistake made on his behalf.

BUT IT TURNED out to be something of a personal triumph, largely thanks to the skills with which Charles himself squared up to his first major public ordeal. An Eistedfodd speech in Welsh had his adopted nation at his feet, drowning out the dissenting murmurs of Plaid Cymru, the Welsh nationalist party, with the Mayor of Caernarvon standing up to declare: 'That wasn't just a boy. That was a Prince. You could have put a suit of armour on him and sent him off to Agincourt.' Even more significantly, he had given his first round of newspaper, radio and TV interviews, in which he emerged for the first time as a relaxed, witty, likeable figure, able to laugh with anyone else at the occasional absurdities of his royal life. During his statutory stint in the services (which he ended, for once outpacing his father, with a naval command of his own), he began to found a series of trusts for charitable, youth and environmental work around Wales and the rest of the United Kingdom, which soon began to spread their work around the Commonwealth. He began to travel abroad. Suggestions from the highest circles that he 'clinched' an £11-million export deal in Brazil may be unconvincing, but in Japan he certainly

REX FEATURES LTD.

LOOKING UNCANNILY LIKE HIS GREAT-GRANDFATHER, KING GEORGE V, A BEARDED PRINCE CHARLES ENDED HIS NAVAL CAREER AS SKIPPER OF HMS *BRONINGTON*.

did persuade Sony to build a factory in the valleys of the Rhondda – and was able, two years later, to open it himself, bringing much-needed employment to one of Wales's most depressed regions. At last, to himself and those around him, he was feeling his way towards a role in which he could prove himself, and be seen to prove himself, useful.

IF THE NEW Prince of Wales lacked some of the glamour of his immediate predecessors, the future Kings Edward VII and VIII, it was deemed just as well. He may not, pre-Diana, have been a leader of fashion, as were both Bertie and 'David'; he may not have had

Edward VIII's knack of putting people at ease in the royal presence, or Edward VII's instinct for the grand gesture. He may, above all, have seemed rather out of touch with the values of his own generation. But none of this much bothered him. 'If people think me square,' he said in one of his most celebrated early pronouncements, 'I am happy to be thought square.' Having lived all his life in a world of adults – and extremely genteel, predominantly female adults, at that – he had developed a profoundly traditional sense of values, and a driving, almost obsessional sense of duty. He seemed unlikely to be dragging the royal family into the law courts, like his great-great-grandfather; nor did he appear the type, like his great-uncle, to renege on his promises. If Prince Charles repeated King Edward VIII's famous pledge that 'Something must be done' – as, increasingly, he did – then Britain could be rather more confident that it would.

WHERE DIANA liked pop music, Charles enjoyed opera; where she loved discos, he preferred a quiet evening at home; where she was terrified of horses, having fallen off one as a child, Charles was as competitively equestrian as the rest of his family. While Diana enjoyed a giggly gossip with friends her own age, Charles preferred the company of older and wiser men, who took on the role of sages, even seers. If she read at all, she chose romantic novels like those of her step-grandmother, Barbara Cartland; he tried to get through at least two non-fiction books, usually works of history or philosophy, in each busy week of his life. Where she loved the Caribbean sun, he shared his family's penchant for wet, blustery breaks at Balmoral and Sandringham. He was a serious-minded, introspective man now entering his thirties; she was, if anything, young for her sixteen years.

THAT DAY IN A ploughed field in Northamptonshire, an earnest Cambridge graduate met a shy and blushful teenager who had yet to pass any exam, even her driving test. It is small wonder that no-one noticed the Prince take a long second glance at his girl-friend's younger sister.

II

A

PUBLIC

ROMANCE

——— · ———

The British press had been marrying off Prince Charles since he was three years old. In 1952, immediately after his mother's accession to the throne, the first of countless lists of eligible brides appeared in a Sunday newspaper, casting its net around all the European houses as well as the stately homes of England. Of the hundreds of candidates canvassed over the next thirty years, not once – until the late summer of 1980, two years after Charles's visit to Althorp – was the name of Lady Diana Spencer mentioned.

ON HIS THIRTIETH birthday in 1978, Charles was the oldest unmarried Prince of Wales since James Stuart, the Old Pretender in 1718 – apart, of course, from his great-uncle the Duke of Windsor, who forty years earlier had abandoned his throne for the woman he loved. Charles regarded it as something of an achievement to have reached the age of thirty unmarried. It broke all recent royal precedents. The entire royal family around him, including his parents, had married in their twenties, as had every future monarch for 200 years. Of those Princes of Wales who became Kings of England, only Henry V and Charles II were unmarried at thirty, and each of them remained so only two more years.

THE SAME WAS to prove true of Charles. After a decade and more of unremitting pressure from press and public, and more recently from his family and friends, his long hunt for a bride had come to haunt him.

ON HIS THIRTIETH birthday, Charles was living through an uncomfortable period of drift. He was patron or president of some two hundred charities, clubs, committees and learned organizations; he had launched, in embryonic shape, the Prince's Trust, and taken over from Lord Mountbatten the presidency of United World Colleges. But there was no cohesive purpose to his public activities, nor indeed to his private life. With few friends beyond the small circle he could trust, mostly his staff and the back-slapping polo brigade, he remained a solitary and rather confused figure. Few Englishmen of thirty, after all, are still living at home with their parents. Unable to go out on a whim, Charles more often than not found himself alone in the evenings, eating a solitary meal off a tray, with a glass of milk, in front of the television. There were urgent reasons, both personal and constitutional, to find himself a wife.

HE HAD COME close to marriage once or twice in his early twenties. But he had been about to embark on a sustained stint in the Services, which would keep him away from home for the best part of six years, and he did not want to be an absentee husband. By the time he had emerged from the Navy, at the age of twenty-eight, he was still of a mind to prolong his independence. Although thirty was looming on the horizon – the age at which, to his eternal regret, he had once said 'a chap like me' should get married – there had seemed to be no particular hurry. He had two brothers to ensure the succession, and perhaps another thirty years before he inherited the throne. For the first time in his life, moreover, this fundamentally shy figure, embarrassed about his weak chin and jug ears, found he had developed an extraordinary power over women, a kind of *ex officio* sex appeal. It took him by surprise, and he began to enjoy it.

JUST ONE OF THE HAZARDS OF BEING THE WORLD'S MOST ELIGIBLE BACHELOR.

FOR THE NEXT few years the Prince of Wales, wherever he went, played the role of a besieged sex symbol. Girls would giggle and scream at his approach as if he were a pop star, lunge forth with kisses as if he were a matinée idol, fight to touch him as if he were divine.

He led the life of the world's most eligible bachelor, romantically linked with some of the world's most glamorous women. On the surface, in an awkward sort of way, he seemed to relish it – unless fighting off the public embraces of married women, such as the American television star Farrah Fawcett, or those with otherwise 'unsuitable' life-styles, like the British film actress Susan George. At heart, however, he was always looking for that oft-mentioned English rose (so oft-mentioned that he once caused a diplomatic incident by forgetting to admit the possibility of a Welsh rose), someone who would be as privately loving and supportive as she would be publicly loyal, discreet and conscientious. There just weren't many of them, from the 'right' sort of families, about.

THE LEGAL AND constitutional restrictions on his choice were daunting. Under the 1689 Bill of Rights, enshrined in the 1701 Act of Settlement, by which his family's legal claim to the throne is established, Charles was forbidden to marry a Catholic. He could not marry anyone without the consent of the sovereign, his mother, or both Houses of Parliament, as stipulated by the Royal Marriages Act of 1772 (instigated, ironically enough, by one of his heroes, George III, in an attempt to stop his wayward sons from marrying mere English roses). There could be no question, given his future role as Supreme Governor and titular head of the Church of England, of marrying a divorcee; in this respect, if few others, the public display of morality expected of the British royals had remained unchanged since the abdication crisis of 1936.

ELIZABETH II HAS gently eased the monarchy into the second half of the twentieth century, social values and all, as witnessed by the fact that in 1955 she forbade her sister to marry a divorced man, yet twenty-five years later permitted her to divorce the man she married instead. More recently, she has even permitted her daughter, the Princess Royal, to contemplate divorce. But it could never be allowed to compromise the position of the heir to the throne. There were cries

FOR HER FIRST PUBLIC
OUTING SINCE THE
ENGAGEMENT, A MEETING
WITH PRINCESS GRACE OF
MONACO, DIANA CHOOSES A
DARINGLY LOW-CUT BLACK
DRESS.

of 'Popery' in the House of Commons when rumours spread about a
romance between the heir to the throne and the Catholic Princess
Marie-Astrid of Luxembourg; equally loud protests when he spent
one summer in the company of a young divorcee named Jane Ward;
and intrigued, speculative memories of Wallis Simpson when the
daughter of an American admiral, Laura Jo Watkins, was flown over to
witness his maiden speech in the House of Lords.

BESIDES, THE PRINCE was also compelled to search for a girl
without – as the British like to euphemize it – 'a past'. The future
Queen of England had to be unblemished, *intacta* – not to mince
words, a virgin. This was the hurdle on which many of his previous
girl-friends had tripped throughout the permissive seventies, when
jealous boy-friends would contact gossip columns with revelations
which immediately ruled them out of contention. As he entered his

thirties, Charles was also aware that his bride would have to be considerably younger than himself – young enough to bear him children, the future heirs of the House of Windsor, without the remotest gynaecological risk.

NON-CATHOLIC, NON-DIVORCED European princesses were as thin on the ground as unblemished, blue-blooded English roses in their late teens or early twenties. As the Prince agonized, many of the available candidates began to give up on him and marry his friends, or other members of the ruling or moneyed classes, while they still had the chance. 'Whenever I give a dinner party these days,' the bachelor Prince observed forlornly, 'everyone seems to be getting married.' His worldly-wise father rubbed salt in the wound: 'You'd better get on with it, Charles, or there won't be anyone left!'

THE QUEEN, THOUGH she had never specifically forbidden her son to marry a commoner, had always impressed upon him her wish that the 'purity' of the British blood royal be preserved – or even enhanced – by a marriage into one of the great British or European families. If not someone of royal birth, then his bride should ideally be a girl able to bring good genes to his lineage as much as contentment to his hearth. More his mother than his Queen, in private as in public, Elizabeth II restrained herself from increasing the pressure on Charles by adding her own voice to the chorus of impatience. But he was aware of the public's dismay, and of the increasingly wild rumours: that he would eventually go the way of the Duke of Windsor, that he was interested only in married women, even that he might be homosexual. Something, in those immortal words of the last Prince of Wales, had to be done.

ON 17 JUNE 1977, the day the *Daily Express* exclusively and 'officially' announced his engagement to the Catholic Princess Marie-Astrid of Luxembourg, brushing aside the constitutional obstacles with a few homespun solutions, the Prince chose to deny the story by announcing: 'I have not yet met the girl I want to marry.' As far as he knew, he was speaking the truth. It was almost six months later, in November of that year, that he first took full notice of Lady Diana Spencer, the girl who had lurked in the outer shadows of his life since the very week of her birth.

THE YOUNG DIANA remained in those outer shadows for the best part of three years, while the dashing royal bachelor sowed a few more wild oats. Then, in the summer of 1980, she went to stay at Balmoral, and stood patiently on the banks of the Dee as her Prince demonstrated his prowess at fly-fishing. When it turned out that she too could catch the odd salmon, Charles began to wonder if this enchanting young creature might be able to make the transition to the rarefied world of royalty.

BY THIS TIME Sarah Spencer had fallen by the wayside. Red-haired, vivacious, an ideal escort, Sarah had suffered from anorexia when she and Charles first noticed each other at Ascot in the summer of 1977. The Prince had sympathetically encouraged Sarah back to good health, and they were soon indulging their mutual love of outdoor sports. A Klosters skiing holiday with friends even led to press speculation about the number of bedrooms in their villa. But Sarah insisted

IT WAS WHILE SQUIRING HER OLDER SISTER SARAH (NEXT TO CHARLES) THAT THE PRINCE FIRST MET DIANA.

SYNDICATION INTERNATIONAL

that the relationship was platonic: 'I am not in love with him… and I wouldn't marry anyone I didn't love, whether it was the dustman or the future King of England. If he asked me, I would turn him down.'

MORE HURT THAN annoyed that Sarah had broken the golden rule of never, but never, talking to the press, Charles did not (as reported) 'drop' her as a result; Sarah was a guest of the Queen at Sandringham in the New Year. But she herself now noticed his eye straying to her younger sister. 'They just clicked,' she said of the encounter in the ploughed field. 'He met Miss Right and she met Mr Right.' Sarah Spencer's claim to a footnote in royal history – once she too had married someone else, old Etonian Neil McCorquodale – was that she had brought the future King and Queen together: 'I played Cupid!'

OF THAT HEADY 1980 Balmoral summer, Charles would later say: 'I began to realize what was going on in my mind, and hers in particular.' When he invited Diana back in September, after inundating her London flat with flowers, the press also began to realize what was going on. Thus began the hounding of 'Shy Di', one of the bumpiest recent episodes in the turbulent history of royal relations with the press.

'SHY DI' BRAVES PRESS PHOTOGRAPHERS AS SHE LEAVES HER CHELSEA HOME.

UNKNOWN TO anyone, the couple had been enjoying clandestine meetings that autumn at the Queen Mother's Scottish home, Birkhall. Fleet Street had lost the scent by November, when Diana was spotted at Princess Margaret's fiftieth birthday party at the Ritz Hotel. One of the departing dinner guests informed the waiting newshounds that Lady Diana had sat next to Prince Charles. The approach of his birthday on 14 November, by now a traditional catalyst for tidal waves of marriage rumours, was all the excuse the tabloids needed.

FOR THE NEXT ten days Diana was hounded from pillar to post, with cameramen disguising themselves as roadsweepers outside the Pimlico kindergarten where she worked, even climbing in the lavatory window. If her car stalled, it was front-page news. All eyes were on Lady Di, but the royal birthday came and went without a word. They didn't even spend the day together. Now the disappointment infected even the quality papers: 'The Court Circular that issued from Buckingham Palace last night,' wrote the *Guardian*, traditionally indifferent to the domestic life of the royals, 'was profoundly disappointing for a nation which, beset by economic and political dissent, had briefly believed that the sound of distant tumbrils was to be drowned by the peal of royal wedding bells.'

NOW BATTLE WAS joined in earnest, with Charles himself refuelling the fires by telling reporters outside his Sandringham door: 'Why don't you go home to your wives? You'll all be told soon enough.' Told what? Speculation remounted. The following day, 16 November, the *Sunday Mirror* revealed 'exclusively' that the Prince and Lady Diana had enjoyed two secret late-night rendezvous on the royal train, which had travelled to 'a secluded siding in Wiltshire' to accommodate a princely tryst. Under cover of darkness, the paper suggested, Diana had been 'ushered through a police road block to the waiting train' after 'a 100-mile dash by car from her home in London'.

THIS WAS TOO MUCH. The Palace's indignant denials were dismissed by the paper's editor, who defiantly stood by his story, adding the dubious assertion that it 'in no way reflected badly on Prince Charles or Lady Diana'. For the first time since 1964, when 'intrusive' photographs had been published of Princess Margaret water-skiing, the Queen considered taking a newspaper to the Press Council. But even 'Love in the Sidings', as Fleet Street dubbed the story, was sidelined by the sight of Diana publicly in tears ten days later, after the Press Association quoted her as saying: 'I'd like to marry soon.' She emphatically denied having said any such thing, and wept as she did so. The agency, like the paper, stood by its story, but this time the Palace made no move. It took Diana's mother, her patience at an end, to intervene with an angry letter to *The Times*:

> 'May I ask the editors of Fleet Street whether, in the execution of their jobs, they consider it necessary or fair to harass my daughter daily, from dawn until well after dusk? Is it fair to any human being, regardless of circumstances, to be treated in this way? The freedom of the press was granted by law, by public demand, for very good reasons. But when these privileges are abused, can the press command any respect, or expect to be shown any respect?'

DIANA HAD BECOME expert at either charming the press or dodging them, sending decoys out of the front door of her apartment block while herself slipping out the back, even giving them the slip in traffic. But her daily harassment had now become a matter for discussion in the editorial columns of the quality papers, even in the House of Commons. For the first time in its twenty-seven-year history, the Press Council found itself convened for an emergency meeting with national newspaper editors, where it was agreed that some of the blame must lie with Buckingham Palace. 'Seventy-five per cent of the speculation would die away if the Palace would quietly explain the situation,' the *Guardian* editorialized. The Palace press office should 'plump for open government, rather than cat-and-mouse silences.'

AFTER A BRIEF cessation of hostilities it was again the *Guardian*, now curiously obsessed, who 'exclusively' revealed on 15 December that the engagement would be announced 'today'. It was not. The reason for this sudden revival of interest was a 'summit meeting' held that weekend at Sandringham (according to the tabloids) between the royal family and the Spencers. This, at last, must be it. The Queen would surely take the chance of her televised Christmas Day message to the nation to pass on the happy news.

IT WASN'T, AND she didn't. If truth be known, Charles had not even raised the subject of marriage with Diana until late that November, when they found themselves standing in a cabbage-patch during a secret meeting at the Gloucestershire home of his friends Andrew and Camilla Parker-Bowles. It was not, as yet, a formal proposal – more, in his own words, an 'If I were to ask you, do you think it might be possible?' But it amounted to a commitment, sanctioned in advance by their hostess, who had headed an unofficial committee of Charles's friends to vet potential brides. Diana, she told friends, 'just giggled'; but her answer was never in doubt, for all the Prince's fears that the continued attentions of Europe's paparazzi might prematurely dull her enthusiasm.

STILL, PAST HIS thirty-second birthday, Charles dithered. As speculation reached fever pitch, and the Prince departed on a prolonged trip to India, the situation was becoming impossible for everyone involved. 'Even I don't know what's going on,' complained the Queen, when asked by intimates about her son and heir's latest romance. In England the shy young kindergarten teacher was still being pursued day and night by rampant media; across the world Charles spoke unusually frankly to the journalists travelling with him: 'It's all right for you chaps. You can live with a girl before you marry her. I can't. I've got to get it right from the word go.' At the Taj Mahal, he told photographers: 'I can understand that love could make a man build this for his wife.

THE NEWLY ENGAGED PRINCESS-TO-BE TURNED HEADS (AND HATS) AT ROYAL ASCOT.

One day I would like to bring my own back here.' Then he slipped away from his hosts, his public and his press for a few days trekking in the foothills of the Himalayas, in as much isolation as he could ever find anywhere.

IT HAD BEEN A gruelling trip so far, with several protest demonstrations, a few political incidents, even some deaths among the vast crowds fighting for a glimpse of him. To those around him, who knew him well, the Prince had seemed unusually on edge. When he descended from his weekend in the mountains, however, the rest of the royal party noted a marked change in him: a sudden calm and confidence which seemed to go beyond the mere rigours of a royal tour. 'It was as if,' said one, 'some huge burden had been lifted from his shoulders.' It was as if, agreed others in retrospect, he had been wrestling with a major decision. And so he had.

TEN DAYS LATER, the royal family foregathered for its annual Christmas house party at Windsor. Of all their several and seasonal homes, Windsor is the one least vulnerable to the prying eyes and ears of the press. To the Queen, who spent the wartime years of her childhood there, it is the most private of her residences, and the one she likes to call home. So it was at Windsor that Charles, seizing this psychological advantage, finally told his parents that he was seriously thinking of asking Diana Spencer to marry him. Had he finally made up his mind? No, not quite: he was sure of his own feelings, but not entirely of hers. He needed a few more quiet moments with her, of the kind so hard to arrange with discretion. Would his mother invite Diana to join them at Sandringham over the New Year? Of course, she said, but this time he must not linger too long over his decision. 'The idea of this romance going on for another year is intolerable for all concerned.'

AT SANDRINGHAM it soon became clear what she meant. The world's press was there in force, taking advantage of the public right-of-way which crosses the royal estate, hounding the royals' every

DIANA'S VISIT TO TETBURY,
GLOUCESTERSHIRE BROUGHT
THE WHOLE TOWN ONTO
THE STREETS.

outdoor excursion. In a remarkable flash of temper, unprecedented in her three decades on the throne, Elizabeth II one day rounded angrily on them and shouted 'Oh, I do wish you people would go away!' The atmosphere was scarcely conducive to royal romance.

THROUGHOUT JANUARY, DIANA continued to endure an ordeal by camera and notebook as she travelled to her job in Pimlico. She and Charles managed several secret meetings – at a 'safe' house in central London, at Highgrove and at the Queen Mother's home on the Balmoral estate. Then Diana forced the pace a little by telling him that she planned to flee to her mother's ranch in Australia, for a much-needed break from all the attention, in early February. Charles, who would be away skiing in the meantime, invited her to dine alone with him at Buckingham Palace on 4 February, a couple of evenings before she was due to leave.

AND THERE, AT LAST, he formally proposed. Diana accepted at once, but a still cautious Prince urged her to 'think the whole thing over' in Australia, lest on mature reflection it prove 'too awful a prospect'. With her mother at her side, Diana never wavered. Three years before, she had thought she might see her elder sister crowned Charles's Queen. Now it was all offered to her: the pomp, the privilege, the wealth, the adulation – as well, as Charles was at pains to point out, as the tedium, the loneliness, the frustrations, the loss of privacy. It was, she decided, what she wanted.

THE GIRL-NEXT-DOOR LOOK WON DIANA INSTANT AFFECTION.

ON SATURDAY 21 FEBRUARY, at a secret dinner party at Windsor Castle, Lady Diana Spencer was the Queen's guest of honour at a table crammed with contemporary royalty, gathered to toast the happy couple. Charles had chalked up another in his long list of royal 'firsts': he had become the first Prince of Wales not even to consider, let alone settle for, an arranged marriage. It was decided that the announcement should be delayed no longer.

HAVING DECIDED IN INDIA TO PROPOSE TO DIANA, CHARLES VOWED TO BRING HER BACK TO THE TAJ MAHAL.

MIDSUMMER
TRUMPETS

—— · ——

At 11.00 a.m. on 24 February, the Lord Chamberlain stepped forward at the beginning of an otherwise routine investiture ceremony at Buckingham Palace. The Queen proceeded to blush with pleasure as Lord Maclean told the august throng that Her Majesty had commanded him to read 'an announcement that is being made at this moment':

> It is with the greatest pleasure that the Queen and the Duke of Edinburgh announce the betrothal of their beloved son, the Prince of Wales, to Lady Diana Spencer, daughter of the Earl Spencer and the Honourable Mrs Shand-Kydd.

FIVE MINUTES LATER, in its offices just a mile from the Palace, the Ulster Weaving Company proudly unveiled to the press its ready-made Charles and Diana tea towels. A record company meanwhile announced plans for the reissue of Paul Anka's twenty-year-old hit, *Diana* – older, in fact, than the princess-to-be. The bonanza was on.

LADY DIANA SPENCER was about to become the first Princess of Wales for seventy years, and the first English girl to marry an heir to the throne for more than three hundred. Anne Hyde, elder daughter of the 1st Duke of Clarendon, married the future King James II in 1659; but she died in 1671, fourteen years before James's accession to the throne, and he subsequently married an Italian Catholic princess, Mary Beatrice of Modena. So Diana, should she in time become the forty-eighth Queen of England, would be the first English-born Queen Consort since the reign of Henry VIII, four of whose six wives were English. Her marriage to Charles, set for 29 July, would be the first wedding of a Prince of Wales in London for 118 years.

NOWHERE WAS THE rarity value of these occasions reflected more vividly than on the Stock Exchange, in the City of London, where it was a good day for the curious array of businesses which would benefit. Shares in Royal Worcester china, which would be churning out everything from commemorative mugs to bone china dinner services, jumped 23p to 293p.

FOR THE STAFFORDSHIRE pottery firm of Wedgwood, traditional manufacturers of high-class royal souvenirs of all shapes and sizes, the news came as a 'lifesaver' at a difficult time. The company had been on a three-day week during this low point of the Thatcher years; now it would be back in full production, with overtime.

HOLDINGS IN HOTEL companies and the big West End stores also rose in anticipation of the inevitable influx of tourists. It was, said the chairman of the British Tourist Authority, 'just the fillip the industry needed'. There were smiles in the boardroom of Birmingham Mint, makers of commemorative coins and medallions, and of the Black and Edgington camping group, producers of marquees and – yes – flags. Publishers Eyre and Spottiswoode announced plans for two 'special' Bibles – standard version at £6.95, and £9.95 for the 'superior' imitation leather edition with silver trimmings. But perhaps the most popular of the day's beneficiaries were the breweries,

THEIR ENGAGEMENT ANNOUNCED, THE COUPLE MEET THE PRESS IN HAPPIER CIRCUMSTANCES.

THEIR WEDDING IN 1981 SAW
EVEN GREATER NATIONAL
CELEBRATIONS THAN THE
QUEEN'S SILVER JUBILEE.

one of whom announced a new brand of real ale for the occasion. The chairman of Moss Bros meanwhile expressed relief that the date chosen was late July: 'Any earlier, and all our suits would have been at Ascot.'

THE LORD CHAMBERLAIN had temporarily lifted the usual restrictions on the use of royal faces and insignia for commercial gain, but Liberty's of Regent Street still did the right thing and had their tea towel approved by the Palace. Liberty's 'Charles and Di' headscarves, pure silk of course, would also be a bargain at £15 each. In Stratford-on-Avon, Skycrafts Ltd planned a Charles-and-Di kite – yours for just £2. And Readicut International, a Yorkshire textile firm which had also been on hard times, rushed thousands of do-it-yourself wall-hanging kits into production. Their plans for a Charles-and-Di rug fell foul, however, of the Lord Chamberlain's office. It is not acceptable, they were told, to have people wiping their feet on the royal face.

IN PORTSMOUTH harbour, the minesweeper HMS *Bronington* fired a twenty-one gun salute in honour of its former skipper and his bride. At the Synod of the Church of England, the Archbishop of Canterbury broke into a debate (appropriately enough, on marriage) to pass on the news. One of the regrets of his relatively new role as Archbishop, said Dr Runcie, was that he no longer conducted marriage services; now he had a particularly august one to which to look forward.

IN THE COMMONS, the Prime Minister broke the news to scenes of suitably loyal acclamation, repeated with even more fervour in the Lords. The lone dissenting voice, not for the first or the last time, was that of the crusading republican MP Willie Hamilton, who expressed his dismay that 'we're in for six months of mush'. Mr Hamilton made a more telling criticism later in the day, when the latest unemployment figures showed that Britain's jobless had risen to 2.5 million, a figure unprecedented since the Great Depression of the 1930s. Queen and

Prime Minister, he charged, had 'connived' at the timing of the royal announcement to distract attention from the woes of the Thatcher government.

FOR THE ROYAL WEDDING, said Mr Hamilton, 'there will be no question of cash limits, a 6 per cent pay curb, or worry about the impact on the public sector borrowing requirement. The sky will be the limit. And the British people, deferential as always, will wallow in it. The winter of discontent is now being replaced by the winter of phoney romance.'

CLEARLY, A JULY WEDDING for Charles and Diana would indeed give a morale boost to what otherwise looked like being a long, hot summer for the Thatcher government. Just as England's victory in the 1966 World Cup football finals had given a boost in the polls to Harold Wilson's beleaguered Labour government, so Mrs Thatcher's Conservatives could now look to a patriotic surge among a people anxious for renewed faith in the *status quo*. Thirty-two years

ON HER WEDDING DAY, DIANA MAKES THE FIRST OF MANY APPEARANCES ON THE BALCONY OF BUCKINGHAM PALACE.

earlier, in late 1948, the birth of an heir to the throne had brought some welcome cheer to a depressed, rationed post-war Britain – in particular, to a London still recovering from the Blitz. Now, with that heir's wedding, the wheel had turned full circle.

IN NOVEMBER 1947, a year before Charles's birth, the wedding of Princess Elizabeth to Lieutenant Philip Mountbatten had similarly enlivened the gloomy post-war scene. It provided, in Churchill's words, 'a flash of colour on the hard road we have to travel'. The worst winter in living memory had been seen in 1947, with snow falling solidly from January till March, coal shortages, and the rationing of even such staples as potatoes. 'There are the makings here of immense discontent,' warned the then *Manchester Guardian*. 'The way to recovery runs on a knife edge. Our democratic system has never been put to a harder test.'

NEVERTHELESS, THE PALACE felt bullish enough to turn aside a Treasury proposal for an 'austerity wedding'. Elizabeth had eight bridesmaids in dresses 'spotted with pearls', and mounted police had difficulty keeping the royal procession route clear of people who 'scampered forward laughing and cheering'. Mused the *Guardian* the next day: 'One might have guessed that republicanism had a surer future. But there really does seem to be in most of the human race a profound instinct to single out some few of the species – to differentiate and idealize them, and to make them the object of a loyalty which no process of thought can justify or destroy.'

PLUS ÇA CHANGE. Thirty-three years later, on the announcement of the engagement of the Prince of Wales, the *Daily Telegraph* declared: 'For a nation more than ever starved of symbols of hope and goodness in its public life, the royal example, far from fading, becomes more important… With so many commoners who hate, it matters more than ever that a prince who loves should one day sit upon the throne.'

BUT THE GUARDIAN now returned to its more familiar tones of middle-class indifference: 'A few midsummer trumpets will hardly come amiss… How is one young and happy couple different from the hundreds of others whose engagement yesterday has gone uncelebrated? It is hard to say, except that some things seem natural and some perverse. Not to congratulate the heir to the throne, or be happy that his bride is the lively, handsome woman that she is, would assuredly put us in the second category.'

SHE MUDDLED HIS CHRISTIAN NAMES, BUT THE GREAT DAY OTHERWISE WENT WITHOUT A HITCH.

IN REFLECTING THEIR readers' values, the news pages of that same day's tabloids again demonstrated the extraordinary, unwavering hold of the British monarchy on the imaginations of its subjects. The grave unemployment figures, as Willie Hamilton had feared, were lost in the tide of 'The King and Di', right down to speculation by one fashion editor that the Queen-to-be might bite her nails. The attempted coup in Spain, ably fended off by King Juan Carlos, was as nothing to the Spencers' descent from King Charles II's bastards.

ON CLOSE EXAMINATION by genealogists, Diana's family turned out to be more English than Charles's. 'The real aristocracy in this country,' sniffed the editor of *Debrett's Peerage*, 'is that which existed before the Industrial Revolution, when lots of people who owned factories were given titles. There are only about 150 families in that category, and the Spencers are well towards the top of them... There is nobody in her family of great importance, but they are nice people who live in beautiful houses and have the good fortune to be related to almost every member of the aristocracy.' Family trees were traced back to the crack of doom. The couple's first son, it transpired, would be the first future monarch ever to have been descended from all the British Kings and Queens who had issue; for Diana would bring Stuart blood to the royal line, the only royal blood it lacked, as

DIANA WAS SOON BRINGING HER OWN NATURAL CHARMS TO THE STIFF FORMALITY OF ROYAL PORTRAITS.

well as hereditary links with Charlemagne and Bonnie Prince Charlie, Humphrey Bogart and Rudolf Valentino. Prince Charles, too, could boast Charlemagne among his ancestors, as well as Shakespeare and Count Dracula, El Cid and Genghis Khan. George Washington was the only American president with whom the Prince of Wales could claim ancestral links, while his bride-to-be boasted no fewer than seven, from John Adams to Franklin D Roosevelt.

THROUGH KING HENRY VIII, Charles and Diana were found to be sixteenth cousins once removed; through an eighteenth-century Duke of Devonshire they were seventh cousins once removed. But Diana brought a great deal more than blue blood to the royal escutcheon. The last Princess of Wales, later King George V's Queen Mary, never made a speech or used a telephone in her life. Less than thirty years after her death, the new Princess of Wales would be the first future Queen of England to have once worked for a living. But first, she was forced to confront one final, bizarre test of eligibility. After magazine innuendoes about her sometime relationship with an Old Etonian Army officer, Diana had to stand by and suffer the indignity of her uncle stepping in to defend his niece's honour. 'Lady Diana, I can assure you, has never had a lover,' intoned Lord Fermoy to a group of journalists who thought they had heard everything. 'There is no such thing as her ever having had a past.'

CHARLES'S CHOICE WAS interpreted in royal circles as a victory for the Queen Mother over the forces of Lord Mountbatten, who had made no secret of his hope that the Prince of Wales might marry one of his granddaughters, the Knatchbull girls. In the wake of Mountbatten's death at the hands of the IRA, there had indeed been a brief courtship between the Prince and Amanda Knatchbull, daughter of Lord Brabourne, at whose Caribbean holiday home on the island of Eleuthera Charles had spent several happy vacations. But their mutual affection had never blossomed into love.

CLOSE AS HE HAS BEEN throughout his life to both the Queen Mother and Mountbatten, it was irritating to Charles that his choice of Diana should be so portrayed. But the reasons were not hard to find. Both Diana's grandmothers and four of her great-aunts were or had been attendants at Queen Elizabeth's court. Her father's mother, Countess Spencer, was a Lady of the Bedchamber, and Ruth, Lady Fermoy, Diana's maternal grandmother, has been a lady-in-waiting since 1960, and one of the Queen Mother's closest lifelong friends. Lady Delia Peel, Lady Lavinia Spencer, Lady Katharine Seymour and the Dowager Duchess of Abercorn, Diana's great-aunts, had all held such arcane titles as Women of the Bedchamber and Mistress of the Robes. At the wedding, the Queen Mother would be surrounded by as many Spencers as the bride.

SO IT WAS especially appropriate that Diana's first domicile as a proto-royal was Clarence House, where the Queen Mother would take her in until the ceremony, and quietly give her a crash course in the art of being royal. Diana's life changed with dramatic abruptness. The night before the announcement of her engagement she spent in her Chelsea home, sharing only with her flatmates the morrow's exciting news. At 11.00 a.m. precisely, even as the Palace statement flashed around the world, a cohort of Special Branch detectives took up station outside her front door – and at her side. No longer would she be careering around London in her now famous Mini Metro; that evening it was a royal Rolls-Royce which arrived to take her to dinner with her fiancé and both their grandmothers at Clarence House, which that night became her home. 'Please,' she begged her flatmates

LAUGHTER AFTER THE TENSION: ON HONEYMOON IN THE MEDITERRANEAN, ABOARD HMS *BRITANNIA*.

as she said her tearful goodbyes, 'please telephone me. I'm going to need you.'

THE LAST TIME London had seen the wedding of a Prince of Wales was the spring of 1863, when *The Times*'s court correspondent found much to disapprove of. 'The royal carriages looked old and shabby, and the horses very poor, with no trappings, not even rosettes, and no outriders… The shabbiness of the whole cortège was beyond anything one could imagine.' He denounced 'that singularly ill-appointed establishment known as the Royal Mews', declaring that 'the servants, carriages and cattle selected to convey the Danish princess [Alexandra] through joyful London came from its very dregs.'

THERE WAS NO danger of that in 1981, as Charles himself sat on a planning committee chaired by the Lord Chamberlain. Much to the disappointment of the Dean and Chapter of Westminster Abbey, who had naturally assumed they would be hosting the occasion, it was the Prince's personal decision to hold the ceremony in St Paul's Cathedral – partly because it can seat more people, more because it can also accommodate a full-scale orchestra. He was determined that his wedding should also be a musical feast. Several courtiers tried to talk him out of it, arguing for the more traditional venue at Westminster – closer to the Palace, thus presenting fewer security problems. When he was told that the longer processional route to St Paul's would escalate costs, given the need for far more troops to line it, he said simply: 'Then tell them to stand further apart.'

'A PRINCELY MARRIAGE', wrote Walter Bagehot, the constitutional historian, 'is the brilliant edition of a universal fact, and as such it rivets mankind.' The Prince of Wales's wedding to Lady Diana Spencer was the biggest media event the world had ever seen. Seven hundred million people watched worldwide as both bride and groom showed endearing signs of nervousness: she muddled her husband's forenames, while he made the not insignificant error of endowing her with her own worldly goods rather than his. As the gloriously sunny day went off without a hitch, ending with the first royal kiss ever seen on the balcony of Buckingham Palace, they were universally deemed a fairy-tale couple, openly in love.

IN GIBRALTAR, HMS *Britannia* waited to take them on an extended honeymoon cruise around the Mediterranean, which included a courtesy call on President Sadat of Egypt only a month before his assassination. Britain was still *en fête* when they returned, and a picture session at Balmoral revealed an already very different Diana: effortlessly radiant, her eyes shining, a young woman with the world at her feet. A new generation of monarchy had been launched; but few yet grasped the full significance of this marriage in the changing history of the British crown.

BACK FROM HONEYMOON, AND OPENLY IN LOVE, CHARLES ROMANCES DIANA BESIDE THE RIVER DEE AT BALMORAL.

THE
TENTATIVE
PRINCESS

——— . ———

Within days of her engagement, Diana had sent a conspicuous signal to the watching world that, even as a princess and future Queen, she was determined to be her own woman. She may have chosen to forfeit her independence, her freedom of movement, her anonymity and much of her privacy, but she was not going to surrender her personal identity. On her first public appearance after the engagement was announced, at a reception for Princess Grace of Monaco, she emerged from the royal limousine wearing a very stylish black evening dress – so low-cut as to provoke gasps even from the hardened royal photographers, much more revealing than has ever been the royal way.

CHARLES SMIRKED HIS WAY through the evening, trying not to be caught looking, as if to say all this was nothing to do with him. There were a few tut-tuts, so the nation was led to believe, among more experienced royal females, and Diana's next day at Clarence House certainly included a few words of caution from the most senior of them all. It was a first royal step few have forgotten; and during the ensuing decade, Diana's faithful following has become familiar with the strength of character behind it. But that dress, at the time, signalled the winning inexperience of youth more than an overnight metamorphosis into a brash new royal presence. Before such self-confidence was again to come naturally, there was a long and difficult learning curve to negotiate.

THE WEDDING ITSELF amounted to being pitched in at the deep end. All Diana had to do was avoid tripping up – to smile, wave, be herself, and look as happy as she undoubtedly felt. Somehow, through the predictable ritual of it all, she managed more; she began to communicate to an adoring public something more distinctive, a personal warmth that they found irresistible. Unconsciously, with all the guilelessness of her youth, the new princess had worked a charm

THE GIRL-NEXT-DOOR HAD BECOME A PRINCESS, AND HER HAIRSTYLE WAS COPIED ALL OVER THE WORLD.

beyond the dreams of most public relations men. She had conveyed even to the sceptical that it was fun to be royal.

MORE REMARKABLY, she had avoided alienating those her own age. Though herself blue-blooded, raised in a house bigger than most of the royal residences, she managed to carry the unmistakable air of the prototype girl-next-door, who might any minute awake to find that it had all been the most wonderful dream. To Britons in their teens and twenties, especially those of her own sex, she transmitted a message they had never heard in their lifetimes: you too can be a princess. It brought the monarchy closer to British youth than Charles had ever managed, giving it an appeal to the young unknown for a generation.

THE HOUSE OF WINDSOR hates to be compared to a soap opera, but Diana's arrival on the royal scene injected precisely the same new momentum as the launch of a fresh young female lead in a television series with flagging ratings. It was two generations since the British people had seen a pretty young woman – Lady Elizabeth Bowes-Lyon, the future Duchess of York, Queen and Queen Mother – actually *become* royal, though at the time there was no suggestion that her husband was destined for the throne. It was three generations since Britain had celebrated the marriage of a male heir to the throne. For Diana's contemporaries and their parents, in other words, it was an entirely new experience to watch a fellow subject metamorphose into royalty. The familiar central members of the royal family, for whom they still maintained almost unbounded affection and respect, had all themselves been born royal, or been royal so long that their true

THAT DEFIANTLY DARING BLACK DRESS WAS AN EARLY SIGN OF DIANA'S INDIVIDUALITY.

origins had been forgotten. There was a new edge of excitement about Diana's good fortune which few begrudged her. However misguidedly, her transformation was seen as an affirmation that democratic principles might yet lurk behind hereditary privilege. It could have happened to anyone.

BUT DIANA'S COCOON was a fragile one. Her early popularity was sustained by wearing a permanent expression of surprised happiness, as if she too could not believe her good fortune, and had no intention of abusing it. For a prolonged honeymoon period, she was content to be a visual aid to a streamlined new monarchy, seen but not heard, a mere adjunct to a roadshow already riding high. Though never a calculated or deliberate ploy, Diana's shy, silent innocence generated an astonishing degree of goodwill, more powerful even than the national celebrations which had attended Elizabeth II's Silver Jubilee in 1977. In the month of the wedding the nation exploded in a frenzy of street parties; neighbour, often for the first time, befriended neighbour; not since the Blitz, said the local elders, had they felt such a powerful sense of community. The magic woven by the British Crown – its ability to rally immense tribal loyalty behind an irrational, indefinable cause – was suddenly centred upon a bashful innocent of twenty, whose charms seemingly knew no bounds. Every flutter of her eyelashes, every shy glance from beneath her brows reduced strong men to tears and held the nation in thrall. Diana, it seemed, had single-handedly given the monarchy a much-needed new lease of life.

CHARLES, FOR ONCE, was only too happy to take a back seat. After spending most of his lifetime in an unremitting spotlight, he cheerfully played second fiddle to the new star of the royal screenplay, basking in her reflected glory. It was a curious state of affairs. The heir to the throne, one of the world's richest and potentially most influential men, if never one of its most charismatic, was now deriving an entirely new personal glamour from this winning young creature, not yet twenty-one, whom he had plucked from obscurity to be his

THE HIGHLAND GAMES AT
BRAEMAR GAVE DIANA A
CHANCE TO DAZZLE IN
TARTAN.

bride. Beyond her wedding vows, Diana had spoken barely a hundred words in public, yet already hers was the most familiar face in the world, smiling out from magazine covers from pole to pole.

RATHER AS IF she were a silent-movie star, whose appeal might crumble once she opened her mouth, Buckingham Palace decided to keep things that way, wrapping the new princess in cotton wool as if she were some kind of national doll. She gave no interviews, made no major speeches, merely smiled and blushed her way through every public appearance. And it worked: her public honeymoon lasted a great deal longer than anyone expected. Charles, his parents and their advisers expected the novelty value of the new princess to wear off within a year or two, and warily prepared to brace themselves for the problems attending the spontaneity of youth unused to royal ways. But Diana's public appeal seemed open-ended. There were to be hiccups, even crises, but her popularity would never dim. Within a few years she had established herself in a long chain of opinion polls as one of the most loved of all the royal *dramatis personae*, and thus one of its most inviolate. If the royal family were to sustain its popular appeal through another period of political hardship, when hardline Conservative policies were dividing management from worker, north from south, rich from poor, Diana's ability to cut across class divides would be indispensable.

THE APPEAL OF a new generation is nothing new to the mechanics of royalty. Official biographies invariably pause to shower superlatives on the emergence of royal offspring as brides and grooms, attracting a new wave of warmth to ageing monarchs whose charms have perhaps begun to fade. No such thing could be said of Elizabeth II, sovereign at the time for thirty years, and steadily advancing towards neo-Victorian venerability; but she had reached the point where her people regarded her with perhaps more respect than affection. A burst of uncomplicated emotion about the monarchy would do it no harm at all.

DIANA MAY HAVE been the first new major royal for several generations, but there was one signal difference about the timing of her arrival. This was the first Queen-in-waiting created in the era of modern telecommunications, when the number of newsmen in pursuit of her every sigh multiplied beyond all belief. The Duke of Windsor, the only British monarch ever to write his memoirs, complained wearily about the sketch artists who would lurk behind trees when he and his brothers took a walk through the park, invading their privacy in the cause of relaying the scene to the following day's newspaper readers. Sixty years on Diana had to contend with an incomparably worse, many-headed monster in the shape of countless cameras, both still and moving, from rival news

DIANA BROUGHT A POP STAR LUSTRE TO CHARLES'S PREVIOUSLY SOBER IMAGE.

outlets the world over – all of whom could sell more copies or boost their ratings with the merest glimpse of her. Some, moreover, were more authorized than others. As well as the staff photographers and journalists from established and recognized organizations – the 'Morning, Ma'am, only doing our job' brigade – there arose the ranks of the paparazzi, freelance photographers unbound by any code of royal ethics, any mutually beneficial understandings that official photo-calls were a bargaining chip for subsequent periods of peace and quiet. Nowhere she went, even within the confines of her own various homes, could Diana feel entirely free from the fear that a powerful lens might be lurking in a distant bush, poking through a window, or snooping from a great height.

WHEN SHE BEGAN to feel understandably claustrophobic, that too was news. The British tabloid newspapers were engaged in a prolonged circulation war, which had drastically diluted their professional ethics. The royal family, proven circulation-boosters, had the added advantage of being an easy target for fabricated stories; they rarely answered back, having for years lived successfully by the old political maxim 'Never complain, never explain'. To deny one story would make silence about others sound like confirmation. In the early Diana years, the Queen would make increasing and unprecedented use of the Press Council, the law courts, injunctions and heartfelt protests – but only after the most extreme transgressions, generally by members of her Household staff who had violated their written vow of discretion, and to little lasting effect.

AGAINST THIS background, it became difficult for the British public to pick its way through the jungle of fact and fiction being published about Diana. When two journalists crawled a mile on their bellies through tropical jungle, to take long-distance photographs of the pregnant princess in her holiday bikini, a few tut-tutted; but many more pored over the resulting pictures. Soon bland good news was not enough, and a steady drip-drip of negative stories began to seep into the public consciousness. Diana was lonely and unhappy; she had developed anorexia; she didn't get on with Charles's friends, and vice-versa; she was spending all his money in wild shopping sprees along Knightsbridge, where the Duchy of Cornwall's American Express card was fast reaching its credit limit. She was bored by the royal way of life, dragging Charles back from the annual holiday at Balmoral, shutting herself away from the claustrophobia of palace life behind the headphones of her gold-plated Sony Walkman. Gossip columnist Nigel Dempster called her a 'spoilt monster' who was making her husband's life 'miserable'.

THOUGH EXAGGERATED at the time, the rumours were ominous. Diana does worry constantly about her weight, and did grow painfully thin as she warmed to her new role as a fashion model. She does enjoy shopping, especially for expensive clothes, though more often than not London stores and designers will take their wares to her. She does prefer the sunshine of Majorca, where King Juan Carlos keeps stylish open house (and the Caribbean, where her mother annually rents Richard Branson's $8,000-a-day private island for her daughters and grandchildren) to the bleak summer weather of the Scottish Highlands. Diana has never managed to assimilate the royals' universal fondness for stalking the heather in Wellington boots, relishing everything the Scottish rainclouds can chuck at them, then relaxing in the evenings with a hearty session of charades. The first time she left Balmoral, famously leaving Charles behind her, it was with just two overheard words which became all too public: 'Boring. Raining.'

DIANA'S BOREDOM WITH the less glamorous aspects of her new life became publicly apparent as early as the autumn of 1982, when she turned up five minutes late – after the Queen, an unforgivable breach of royal protocol – at the annual Festival of Remembrance for Britain's war dead. The tabloids squabbled over the details behind the incident, printing sundry versions of an argument

DURING RUMOURS THAT SHE HAD DEVELOPED ANOREXIA, CHARLES UNUSUALLY LET HIS CONCERN SHOW IN PUBLIC.

with her husband loud enough to be passed on by Palace servants. Whatever the truth of the matter, it was but one in a chain of such anecdotes which persuaded the public of a certain, apparent wilfulness on the part of the young new princess – in short, a reluctance to put duty before pleasure without a second thought. She missed her friends; she was acutely lonely in the stiff formality of a world of older, duller adults; she was beginning to experience those very doubts and regrets which Charles had anticipated.

C OULD IT ALL be true? Ten years on, it scarcely seems to matter. The couple's press was to get worse before it got better, and a public hungry for the minutiae of Diana's life found much with which to sympathize in her apparent problems. That a lively young girl suddenly trapped in a gilded cage should find her new life irksome, for all its concomitant privileges, only made her the more endearing. As she continued to grace public occasions with a smile, eagerly responding to a growing public fascination with her clothes and her hairstyle, there was enormous fellow-feeling around the land.

DIANA'S SMILE WON
AUSTRALIAN HEARTS...

T HIS , THOUGH RARELY rationalized, is another essential function of the modern domestic monarchy. Britons of all classes and degrees feel entitled to sit around at home, in pubs or in restaurants discussing the most intimate details of the life of the royal family as freely as they would their own. Probably, in many cases, more freely. If the Queen and other members of the royal family find this unsettling, even distasteful, they are also forced to acknowledge that it is merely another sign of the powerful psychological hold this extraordinary institution exercises over its subjects. And the Queen, to be blunt, has only herself to blame.

IN 1969, AT THE time of Prince Charles's investiture at Caernarvon, Elizabeth II allowed herself to be persuaded to sanction a television film about the Royal Family's life, both on and offstage. Her then press secretary, an imaginative young Australian named William Heseltine – later, as Sir William, to become her private secretary – overcame the Queen's doubts about the wisdom of the enterprise. Close to her heart, after all, was the most celebrated pronouncement of Walter Bagehot, the Crown's most eloquent twentieth-century apologist: 'We must not let in daylight upon magic.' Thus, he argued, might the monarchy's mystique begin to crumble.

ROYAL FAMILY, A joint BBC-ITV enterprise first screened throughout Britain and the Commonwealth the night before the investiture, was an enormous popular success. For the first time in history, Britons were permitted to peep into the private lives of their royals, to see them at play as well as at work. The next day's pomp and ceremony was thus viewed in an entirely new context: Prince Philip, solemnly looking on in his Field Marshal's uniform, had last been seen rowing his youngest son into a Scottish sunset; the Prince of Wales, now declaring himself his mother's 'liege man of life and limb', had reduced his brother to tears by snapping a cello string in his face; and the majestic hands which now placed a coronet on her son's head had last been seen wielding a Balmoral barbecue fork. The royals may not quite have been a family like any other; but for the first time they were very powerfully demonstrated to be a family, who did relatively normal things in relatively normal ways.

...AND CANADA LOVED HER YOUTHFUL *JOIE-DE-VIVRE*.

THE ERA OF the cosy domestic monarchy had been born. In the subsequent twenty years, the popularity of the institution has been considerably shored up by this dramatic new approach – which would have been anathema, no doubt, to previous generations. But its success has been double-edged. The voyeuristic fascination engendered by that film has since created an insatiable appetite around the world for the flimsiest titbits of royal gossip. As the royals have continued to use television for their own ends – virtually every member of the family, notably the Prince of Wales, has now hosted everything from documentaries to game shows – they have begun to deprive themselves of the right to complain about 'intrusion' into their private lives. The royal relationship with television and the newspapers has thus become dangerously ambiguous. They need the media as much as the media need them; but the royals are increasingly being forced to realize, somewhat to their surprise, that they cannot always dictate their own terms.

DIANA HAS BEEN the main beneficiary of this syndrome, and its main victim. Shrewdly, she has rarely herself complained about press misconduct, leaving others to make indignant protests on her behalf. But it is usually the writers who have caused offence; the photographers, the majority of whom behave by an unwritten set of royal rules, have made her the global superstar she undoubtedly enjoys being. The Princess has a film star's love of the camera, and a model's advantage of being extraordinarily photogenic. It is almost impossible to take a bad picture of her.

IN HER EARLY years as a princess, a nervous Diana sometimes had to be persuaded by Charles to turn out for the cameras – as, for instance, on their first skiing trip together, which she was innocent enough to think of as a private holiday. It was not long, however, before she began to respond eagerly to the presence of cameramen, at times almost flirting with them. The vast array of different images of her throughout this book, the work of just one fine photographer over that decade, is itself symbolic of the multi-faceted icon she willingly became. For a young woman whose face appeared so frequently in newspapers and magazines, it was revealing to discover that, for her, the thrill did not wear off.

D I D D I A N A misunderstand what it meant to be a princess? Did she believe that her lofty new status was akin to that of a film star, a magazine cover girl, rather than an incarnate symbol of national stability and security? There emerged critics who believed so. Even they had difficulty defining precisely the mystical powers required of a future Queen; but they were certain that it did not amount simply to maintaining a consistent presence in the annual lists of the World's Best Dressed Women.

W I T H I N M O N T H S O F her reincarnation as a royal, however, even as the seeds of this agonized debate were being sown, the Princess of Wales presented the nation with news stirring enough to disarm all criticism.

ON THEIR FIRST SKIING HOLIDAY, A RELUCTANT DIANA HAD TO BE PERSUADED BY CHARLES TO FACE THE CAMERAS.

V

'AN
HEIR
AND A
SPARE'

——— · ———

It was in May 1948, less than six months after her marriage to the former Prince Philip of Greece and Denmark, that the rumours about Princess Elizabeth began. On an official visit to Paris she seemed, according to the French newspapers, 'tired and listless'. At a British Embassy reception in her honour that evening, she had met only half the guests when her husband led her from the room to rest. On 4 June, the eve of Derby Day, a Buckingham Palace statement, coyly avoiding the word 'pregnant', announced that 'Her Royal Highness Princess Elizabeth, Duchess of Edinburgh, will undertake no public engagements after the end of June.'

E L I Z A B E T H G A V E the nation – and her husband – what they wanted, a male heir in direct line of succession to the throne, six days before her first wedding anniversary. Thirty years later, it was another unenviable royal precedent for that same son and his bride to confront. In quite as short a time, England expected Diana to be expecting.

T R U E T O F O R M, she did not disappoint them. The royal couple enjoyed a triumphant tour of their principality, during which even Diana managed to stammer a few words of Welsh, before tentative arrangements for Commonwealth visits of the kind expected of them had to be put on hold. The fairy-tale aura still surrounding the Princess was further enhanced by the news that, within a matter of months, she had become pregnant.

DIANA'S FIRST PREGNANCY CONTINUED HER PERSONAL FAIRY-TALE...

PRINCE WILLIAM Arthur Philip Louis was born on 21 June 1982, more than a month ahead of the royal schedule set by Diana's in-laws. The fact that her first child was a boy, a prince who would one day succeed his father on the throne, again added to Diana's apparent ability to meet every royal challenge, however bizarre, placed in her path. For Charles, the birth of a son was a huge weight off his shoulders. In two years he had made up all the ground which had seemed so intractable as he had entered his thirties; he had provided the nation with a future Queen whose popularity knew no bounds, and he had ensured the succession. For the Queen, too, William's arrival provided constitutional delight as much as natural joy at the birth of her third grandchild.

IN WHAT WAS fast becoming her trademark fashion, Diana again dispensed with royal precedent by choosing to have her baby in hospital. In a private ward of a private hospital, of course – but the potent symbolism of an ever more modern monarchy was not lost on mothers the nation over. Charles had been born in a specially equipped maternity ward inside Buckingham Palace; the Queen had been born at her parents' home in London, Princess Margaret at her mother's ancestral family seat, Glamis Castle in Scotland. William was the first future King of Britain to have been born, like the vast majority of his future subjects, in a hospital bed.

THE SPEED WITH which the monarchy appeared to be adapting to the times may have been accelerated by Diana; but in the matter of royal births, she was moving in an area of unusual public potency, until recently locked in unbelievably outmoded tradition and practice.

...AND GAVE HER A CHANCE TO SHOW THAT EVEN MATERNITY CLOTHES CAN BE STYLISH.

EVEN KING GEORGE VI, the most traditional of monarchs, had baulked at the custom whereby the Home Secretary of the day was required to be present at all births in potential line of succession to the throne. The practice dated back to 1688, when James II's wife, Mary of Modena, was accused of producing a changeling as heir to the throne (known to popular history as 'the warming-pan baby'), despite the presence of the Lord Chancellor and all available Privy Councillors at the foot of her bed. In more recent times it had led rather to embarrassment and farce. In 1926 the then Home Secretary, William Joynson-Hicks, had waited uneasily downstairs at 17 Bruton Street, Mayfair, during the Caesarian section that delivered Princess Elizabeth – even though her father, at the time, had no expectation of becoming King. Four years later his successor, J R Clynes, summoned early to Glamis because of a false alarm, spent two weeks kicking his heels at Airlie Castle and was finally in mid-dash between the two when Princess Margaret was born.

PRINCE WILLIAM ARTHUR PHILIP LOUIS WAS BORN WITHIN A YEAR OF THEIR MARRIAGE.

BARELY THIRTY YEARS after such flummery had finally died the death, a new Princess of Wales was instinctively aiding her mother-in-law's inch-by-inch policy of bringing the monarchy gently down to earth, removing the more absurd aspects of its remoteness from the normal lives of its people. Diana, moreover, had herself been a kindergarten teacher; she and Charles were known to dote on children (unlike his sister Anne, who has confessed to a shortage of 'normal' maternal instincts). In an age when controversy raged over attitudes to, even methods of, childbirth, the royal family believe that they have an important example to set. It was for this reason, for instance, that Princess Elizabeth let it be known in 1948 that she was breastfeeding the infant Prince Charles, though forced by influenza to give up after only two weeks. At the time, when Cow & Gate advertised itself as 'the milk of princes', this was regarded as something of a royal watershed. The Princess believed so strongly in the virtues of breastfeeding that she was prepared to defy the powerful taboo surrounding any mention of royal anatomies.

AT WILLIAM'S CHRISTENING, THE QUEEN WAS AS DELIGHTED AS CHARLES THAT THE SUCCESSION WAS ASSURED.

A GENERATION ON, the breastfeeding debate had been won, and Diana needed no special dispensation to follow the example of the vast majority of British motherhood. There were other innovations she wished to make, however, which confronted other royal taboos, reminding her that she was no longer in a position to bring up her children entirely as she wanted. When the couple's postponed tour of Australia was rescheduled, following her safe delivery, the Queen privately tried to talk Diana out of her expressed wish to take her baby with her. Royal tours were more arduous than perhaps the Princess realized. The logistics were immensely complex; even if she took a fleet of nannies along, which would add to the

WILLIAM'S FIRST PHOTO-CALL WAS HELD IN THE GROUNDS OF GOVERNMENT HOUSE, AUCKLAND, NEW ZEALAND.

expense, she would still be able to spend very little time with her child. But Diana kept her foot down, and it was typical of the Queen's shrewdness in matters domestic and constitutional that she decided to let her headstrong daughter-in-law learn by her mistakes.

THUS IT CAME to pass that Prince William's first official photo-call since his christening took place on the lawn of Government House in Auckland, New Zealand, where the press photographers escorting the royal tour were delighted to have an unusual scoop on their hands. But Diana was beginning to see the wisdom of the Queen's words. Besotted with her son, she found the constant partings hard to take as the tour wore on, and she could see that it unsettled the child to be constantly trans-

BACK AT KENSINGTON PALACE, THE FUTURE KING WAS SOON PROVING A HANDFUL.

ported from one strange new bed to another. Many royal tours lay ahead in the coming months and years, but this was the last on which she would take him along. The best to be said about Diana's misjudgement is that it was a very sympathetic one, especially in the eyes of the people of Australia and New Zealand, who were delighted by an apparently unprecedented gesture towards them. Furthermore, she avoided the shower of criticism which was to befall Britain's next new princess, her close friend Sarah Ferguson, when six years later she left a very young first child behind her to make an extended, only partly official trip to her husband's side in the Pacific.

THE IMMEDIATE period after William's birth was a very busy one, with Charles intent on introducing Diana to as much of the Commonwealth as possible; so the couple might well have taken considerably longer to provide the royal family with what even they call 'an heir and a spare'. Prince Henry Charles Albert David, to be

known as Harry, in fact arrived on 15 September 1984, only two years and three months after his brother. Another wave of national euphoria staunched growing tabloid insinuations about the marriage, but not for long. The British people had been fed a diet of pap to the effect that Charles and Diana were 'thoroughly modern' parents who would bring up their children in a more 'natural' way than either of them had themselves known in their own very different childhoods. When Charles began to absent himself more than most fathers, however busy their professional lives, eyebrows were raised. There was no doubt that Diana was a devoted and dedicated mother, but was Charles playing a sufficient role in the lives of his young sons?

OVER THE NEXT three years, public concern was fed by a tidal wave of negative publicity which the Palace handled about as effectively as King Canute. The truth which gradually began to emerge was that Charles and Diana really were the products of very different worlds, to an extent forgotten by devotees now accustomed to regarding them as a single royal unit. The Prince, more than his evident soft-heartedness might suggest, thought it entirely natural for children to be brought up in the traditional royal way: at the hands of schoolteachers and nannies, to learn to know their place, and never to get in the way of paternal pursuits and inclinations. It came as a surprise; and a stark reminder that there are limits to the extent to which Charles – who has tried more than any other member of his family to see how the other half lives – can ever really escape from the straitjacket imposed by his birth.

W HEN THE YOUNG princes began their schooldays, it was clear that Charles was keen to repeat the pattern of his own education, out in a world as real as the royals ever get to see. Diana was an assiduous and involved parent, taking part with a will in the mothers' race, and often herself taking the children to their London day school in the mornings, or picking them up at the end of the day. The Prince was less in evidence at the school gates, but then so are many busy fathers. Prince William was reputed to be a bit of a tearaway – publicly spanked, on one occasion, by his mother (inevitably causing a prolonged national debate about the merits of corporal punishment) – but then so are many firstborn children. The difference for these parents and children was that they were obliged to live so much of their lives in the remorseless glow of incessant, often ill-informed, public scrutiny.

DIANA IS GRIMLY DETERMINED TO WIN THE MOTHERS' RACE AT WILLIAM'S LONDON DAY SCHOOL.

IT IS LIKELY that Charles and Diana will have to live with negative rumour and speculation for years to come, whatever public face they choose to show to the world. For the royals, there is nothing new about that. Buckingham Palace has in its time chosen to deny rumours of rifts in the Queen's marriage, though curiously it has never ventured to issue any such statement about the Prince and Princess of Wales, even at the height of the direst publicity.

HAPPILY, HOWEVER, the worst now seems behind them. It climaxed in 1987, which also saw the royal couple involved in tragedy on the ski slopes of Klosters, where an avalanche killed a close friend and nearly swept away the Prince of Wales. Since then, with typical defiance, the private Prince has continued to take his separate excursions – to fish in Scotland, paint water-colours in Italy, trek the Kalahari desert with his elderly mentor, Sir Laurens van der Post. Such separations have thus taken on the appearance of routine, rather than emergency. An anxious British people has grown accustomed to the fact that this is not, in the final analysis, a marriage like any other. Nor could it ever have been.

THE ONE STRIKING result is that Charles and Diana have now adopted very different, and separate, public personae. Their match was expected to blend them into a couple who would in many ways symbolize the nation's future; instead they have taken on this burden in identifiably distinct ways. Their public appearances together are surprisingly rare, usually reserved for family or state occasions. If it is largely taken for granted that Prince Philip escorts the Queen on the majority of her public appearances, the same is no longer true of the next generation. The affection and respect in which they are both held is thus much more the product of the public work they do, than simply the result of who they are.

THEIR CHILDREN, sensibly, have as yet been seen no more than absolutely necessary. If ever there is a time when royalty deserves to be protected from undue disruption and scrutiny, it is in childhood.

The rest of their lives will be lived publicly enough. The great royal 'experiment' in sending Prince Charles to school nearly had to be abandoned more than once, when undue invasion of his privacy threatened the education of his school-fellows as much as his own. With this in mind, the Prince and Princess have gone to the lengths of entertaining all national newspaper editors to lunch individually, in the hope of persuading them to spare their children yet awhile. It has

not always worked; a 'paparazzi' photograph of a new nanny wheeling a new pram appeared on the front page of the *Daily Mirror* the very morning after its editor had attended just such a lunch. News values, incomprehensible though it may seem to the victims, can overmaster even a royal command. On the whole, however, the characters of William and Harry remain to be revealed to us, which is precisely as it should be.

N O W T H A T they have weathered those early storms, moreover, the Prince and Princess of Wales reach their tenth wedding anniversary presenting a happy and united face to a people who will hear little wrong of them. But the celebrations are likely to engender another new pressure they have so far escaped. Having ensured the succession with the births of Prince Charles and Princess Anne, the Queen went on

JUST WILLIAM UP TO MISCHIEF AT SANDRINGHAM.

ON RICHARD BRANSON'S
PRIVATE CARIBBEAN ISLAND,
DIANA AND HARRY ENJOY A
SECLUDED MOMENT OF THE
KIND SO RARE BACK HOME.

to have two more children in the second decade of her marriage, giving birth to Prince Edward in her thirty-eighth year. Royalty traditionally enjoys, and is expected to enjoy, raising large families. Charles himself, in his self-styled role as an 'incurable romantic', is known to share this as so many other of his family's in-built inclinations.

DIANA HAS turned thirty a month before the anniversary. Whatever her own private feelings, it seems inevitable that her position, her in-laws and her husband – not to mention public demand – will require her to bear at least two more children in the decade ahead. This time, it will be a very different princess who conforms to the royal rules. In the six years since the birth of her second son, Diana has had the chance to build a public persona scarcely recognizable as the 'Shy Di' who beguiled Britain through the early 1980s. These will be the children of a mature, respected and accomplished princess with her sights firmly set on the twenty-first century.

A SUMMER FORTNIGHT AT KING JUAN CARLOS'S MAJORCAN RETREAT IS NOW PART OF THE FAMILY'S ANNUAL CALENDAR.

VI

AT HOME

——— · ———

Prince Charles's first act of each day is to jot down his dreams on the notepad beside his bed. 'You can learn an awful lot from your dreams,' says the philosopher prince, who will then switch on BBC Radio 4's farming programme.

DIANA, MORE OFTEN than not, will already be up. As Charles steps into the bath drawn by one of his valets, his wife will usually be in the pool at Buckingham Palace, completing her statutory stint of morning lengths. They will meet up again over Lapsang Souchong tea, accompanied by some fruit, maybe even toast, before their paths divide – Diana perhaps to take Harry to school, if her schedule permits, Charles to prepare for his morning meeting with his private secretary. Though coiffed daily by her loyal hairdresser, Richard Dalton, the Princess will do her own make-up before squaring up to the demands of the day. It will be a rare one on which she sees her husband again before the evening.

THUS BEGINS THE average working day in Apartments 8 and 9 of Kensington Palace, the royal 'ghetto' the Waleses share with Princess Margaret, the Gloucesters, and Prince and Princess Michael of Kent. A typical day will continue with Charles receiving civic or foreign dignitaries, or representatives of one of the many trusts and charities busy in his name, while Diana plays a set of tennis at the Vanderbilt Club in Shepherds Bush before lunch with a friend and an

AFTER DROPPING HARRY AT SCHOOL, DIANA CHATS WITH ANOTHER PARENT.

afternoon engagement. The Princess will always try to be at home for bathtime and bedtime with her children. If she has the evening off, she may well slip out on her own (apart from her ubiquitous detective)

– to the ballet, the opera, a private meal with friends, perhaps even a cinema.

ONCE OR TWICE a month the couple will host a large, perhaps star-studded dinner party, where rock stars like Phil Collins or Bob Geldof may find themselves sitting next to a cabinet minister or the Archbishop of Canterbury. If Charles is having a group of his more highbrow friends to dinner, Diana may well excuse herself and eat separately with chums her own age.

ANOTHER NEIGHBOUR in Kensington Palace is her older sister Jane, whose husband, Sir Robert Fellowes, has recently become the Queen's private secretary. Also a couple with a thirteen-year age gap, Jane and Robert are among Charles and Diana's closest friends, able as they are to share many of the royal intimacies which make other friendships so difficult. To be more than an acquaintance of royalty requires a rare combination of virtues beyond a respectable pedigree – above all, utter discretion. One word out of place, let alone to the newspapers, spells banishment from the royal circle. Diana has had to fight to retain some of the friendships which preceded her marriage, and which offer welcome light relief from the rigours of her *vita nuova*; Carolyn Bartholomew, one of her Chelsea flatmates, and Mervyn Chaplin, a friend since their teens, are among the few to have remained close to her throughout the decade.

WITHIN THE FAMILY, Charles remains closer to his mother than his father. Early in his marriage, while Diana was still feeling her way, he relied on the Queen for the kind of personal advice and

A WINDSWEPT WELCOME FROM POST OFFICE WORKERS IN NORTH LONDON.

HER PATRONAGE RAISES
MUCH-NEEDED FUNDS FOR
MEDICAL RESEARCH...

encouragement available from so few other sources. He has always been a rather distant older brother to Andrew and Edward, who are much closer to Diana. The Princess has also established a warm and jokey relationship with Prince Philip, who shares, after all, the experience of having married a spouse who must always walk a pace or two ahead. The Queen is delighted by the Princess's public success, and her talents as a hard-working, conscientious mother; but relations between them remain cordial rather than affectionate. It is Fergie, Duchess of York, who goes out riding with the Queen, relishing her new place at the royal hearth, while Diana frankly prefers whenever possible to escape to the company of friends who do not double as courtiers.

THE PRINCESS personally hires and fires the domestic staff, notably the royal nannies, who tend to have a relatively high turnover rate. Like most working mothers, Diana is anxious that no surrogate should take her place in her sons' affections. In many other ways, she manages to relax the stiff formality of the world into which she married. Few royal mothers before her, for instance, have encouraged the children to climb into the royal four-poster in the mornings – as Harry, apparently, still does from time to time, especially if his father is not there. It is no secret that separate bedrooms are another price of royal life; Charles will often sleep apart, in his dressing room, if he has been working late or has an early start the next morning.

APART FROM THE Queen herself, Charles and Diana are the hardest-working members of the royal family, undertaking some five hundred public engagements between them per year. It is no idle sycophancy to say that each prefers to be actively involved in a cause close to their hearts rather than mere names on a letterhead. Diana is patron of forty-four charities, making some two hundred solo visits a year on their behalf, immeasurably increasing their ability to raise funds. She has recently taken on heavy-duty social issues such as homelessness and drug abuse.

SO WARM AND genuine is Diana's public face that she can charm even the least fortunate of Britons, those most likely to resent the privilege and creature comforts which go with her rank. 'The patients always remark afterwards how human she is,' said Debbie Newbury of Turning Point, a charity dealing with drug abuse. 'One client said he felt like he was talking to his sister.'

DIANA'S WORK ON behalf of AIDS vicitims is an especially striking example of the potent symbolism at royalty's command. When she opened Britain's first full-time AIDS ward, and conspicuously removed her gloves to shake hands with victims of the virus, the Princess did more to dispel the fears of a confused and alarmed public than millions of pounds' worth of government advertising.

SHE IS THOROUGHLY briefed before each public appearance, and is visibly becoming more confident (after a rather shaky start) at making short, pertinent speeches. Though she took lessons in public speaking from the film director Sir Richard Attenborough, she has since perfected a style which seems to come straight from the heart. As patron of Relate, formerly the Marriage Guidance Council, Diana has

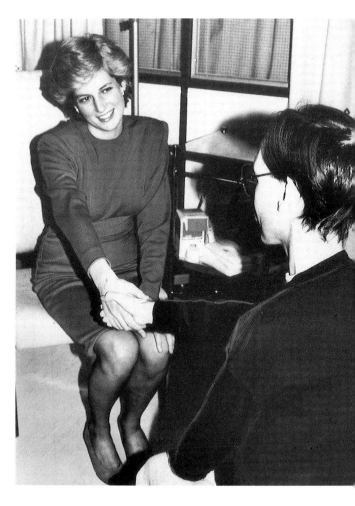

...AND SHE HAS SHOWN PARTICULAR CONCERN FOR VICTIMS OF AIDS.

attended training sessions in which counsellors acted out the roles of arguing couples. In February 1990 she gave an address to a 200-strong audience at Relate's Family of the Year ceremony. 'Marriage offers stability, and maybe that is why nearly seven thousand couples a week begin new family lives of their own... Sadly, for many, reality fails to live up to expectations. When that happens, most couples draw on new reserves of love and strength.'

SEAN CONNERY MEETS HIS FUTURE KING AT ONE OF THE FILM PREMIERES WHICH RAISE MONEY FOR THE PRINCE'S TRUST.

EVERY PUBLIC STEP the royal couple take will have been trodden before them by an advance team from their private office – a private secretary, a press secretary, a security officer. The planning for each visit includes a 'recce' of every outside location by this soft-spoken, pin-striped team, who will have walked the royal route, vetted the guest list, and briefed those to be introduced on the curious protocols of meeting royalty. Never, for instance, reach out to shake a royal hand; wait for it to be extended towards you. When talking to the Prince of Wales, never refer to the Queen as 'your mother'. Do not smoke in the royal presence. Make sure a lavatory is available at a level above the ground floor.

IN 1987, ON THE recommendation of a firm of management consultants, the Prince of Wales's Office was moved from Buckingham Palace to St James's Palace, where it is manned by a small, ill-paid staff headed by a private secretary and two assistants. Here, too, Diana has a tiny but devoted team helping to deal with her mountainous mail, including more requests for an appearance than the rest of the royal family combined. Despite the huge scale of the international media demands upon them, Charles and Diana are allotted no press secretary of their own; their affairs are handled by one of the two assistant press secretaries to the Queen, based in Buckingham Palace.

THE COUPLE THUS live in one palace, maintain their office in a second and their press headquarters in a third, which would seem the perfect recipe (as it can sometimes prove) for administrative chaos. To make matters worse, the royal roadshow moves on at weekends, and as much as possible during the school holidays, to Tetbury in Gloucestershire, where the couple maintain what they regard as their real home.

THE DUCHY OF Cornwall purchased Highgrove for Charles, purely as a country house, before he was married. The former home of the late Maurice Macmillan MP, son of the Conservative prime minister, it is the tranquil oasis to which he and his wife retreat from their royal workload. It amounts, perhaps, to the nearest to a 'real world' that they can build for themselves.

ONLY THE MOST privileged of friends and advisers are invited down the M4 to Highgrove. Most of the real work of monarchy goes on in London, where the couple unite their separate staffs for twice-yearly planning meetings, charting the course of their activities for the six months ahead. Over a map of Britain are laid layers of plastic recording their movements in recent years; the heap of invitations to be evaluated are weighed against the regions where a visit is overdue. Very rarely can the royals agree to a spontaneous, short-notice request; usually it will take a major disaster, such as the Zeebrugge ferry tragedy or the Welsh floods of recent years, to see them drop everything and rush to the scene.

CHARLES AND DIANA REGARD HIGHGROVE, THEIR COUNTRY RETREAT IN GLOUCESTERSHIRE, AS THEIR REAL HOME.

IN BUCKINGHAM Gate, directly across the road from Buckingham
Palace, is a handsome Pennethorne building which houses another of
Charles's offices: the headquarters of the Duchy of Cornwall, source
of his income and a major demand upon his time. The Duchy owns
some 130,000 acres in twenty counties, more than half of it farmland;
other assets range from Dartmoor Prison to the Oval cricket ground.
Landlord to some five thousand people in south London and the West
country, the Prince has devoted much energy over the last two decades
to long overdue reform of the estates and their management, himself
fast becoming an authority on the complexities of agricultural
development and land reform. His rural tenants regard him as a
sympathetic and enlightened landlord, who will drop in unexpectedly
from time to time. One of his tenant-farmers even enjoyed the Prince
as a house-guest for a few nights, with the specific purpose of learning
how to milk cows. He had good reason. 'Two-thirds of Prince
Charles's income', as one Duchy executive put it, 'comes out of the
udder of a cow.'

THE DUCHY'S NET profits, which go straight into Charles's
pocket, have recently averaged in excess of
£2 million a year. In his youth, following a
practice instituted by the Duke of Windsor, he
surrendered 50 per cent to the Treasury as
a voluntary form of income tax; since his
marriage, he has reduced this to 25 per cent.
This hereditary income makes Charles, according to a recent survey by *Money* magazine, the
fourteenth wealthiest individual in Britain,
with assets totalling some £350 million.

BY NATURE, HOWEVER, he is chronically
spendthrift, often nagging his staff about petty
expenditures and worrying about domestic
bills. The Queen, the world's richest woman, is

'TWO THIRDS OF HIS INCOME
COMES OUT OF THE UDDER
OF A COW.'

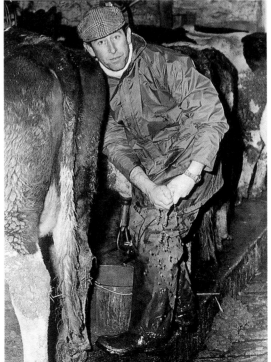

THE WESTERN MORNING NEWS CO. LTD.

said to walk around the corridors of Buckingham Palace last thing at night, switching off all the lights. Charles has emulated his mother by negotiating deals with fashion designers to provide his wife – the best walking advertisement available – with goods at cost price or less. One of the few personal extravagances he does permit himself, to the tune of an estimated £50,000 a year, is

THE ROYAL COUPLE INTERRUPTED THEIR SCHEDULE TO VISIT FLOOD VICTIMS IN CAERNARVON.

maintaining the string of ponies required to indulge his favourite off-duty passion, polo.

INTRODUCED TO THE game by his father, Charles has taken to polo with even greater fervour. In his youth he played for Young England, and experts believe he could have been a world-class player if his duties had permitted him more time to practise. To the Prince, polo represents an escape from the frustrations of so much of the rest of his life, clogged as it is by bureaucracy, red tape and the constant inhibitions of royalty. To watch him play is to see another side of his character on stark display: a dogged determination to win which will have him fighting for possession of the ball, or heading into challenges, with a passionate, almost reckless zeal. The accident in June 1990 which broke his right arm in two places, and effectively ended his polo career, seemed almost inevitable; he was lucky it had not happened earlier. As with skiing, which nearly claimed his life in 1988, Charles takes on the maximum risks with more determination than skill. He is more than competent at both sports, but not quite talented enough for some of the challenges he sets himself.

MOST MEN, HOWEVER regretfully, realize there are things they must give up upon reaching the age of forty. Not Prince Charles, fired

by his father with a fierce com-
petitive spirit, and by his own
strength of character with a
determination to prove himself
worthy of all the attention paid
him. In the late 1970s a series of
spills forced him to give up
steeplechasing, and abandon his
dream of riding in the Grand
National; but he remained reluc-
tant to admit the plain truth that, like the last Prince of Wales, he
simply wasn't a good enough horseman. In the 1930s the government
of the day became so alarmed by Prince Edward's recklessness on
horseback that the prime minister begged the King to intervene
before he broke his neck; similarly, in recent years, Charles's series of
accidents have reopened the debate about the freedom of an heir to
the throne to indulge in dangerous sports. No-one would wish to deny
the usual personal freedoms to a man already hedged around with
enough restrictions; on the other hand, given the national investment
of time, money and goodwill in the heir to the throne, he has a
constitutional duty to reach that throne intact.

FOR MOST OF HIS adult life Charles has been almost obsessive
about polo, fitting in at least one game a week even when abroad on
official tours of duty. While Diana has taught their sons to swim and
play tennis, Charles has given them riding lessons (though his failure,
as yet, to take them fishing has caused some surprise). In May 1990,
shortly before the accident which permanently damaged his right
arm, the boys were taken by their nanny, Jessie Webb, to watch their
father playing polo. Soon they began to play their own makeshift game
on the touch line. Between chukkas, Charles shouted 'Come here!'
and gave each of them a kiss on the head. It remains one of the very
few public displays of affection he has permitted himself.

IT WAS A GREAT BLOW TO
CHARLES WHEN HIS POLO-
PLAYING CAREER WAS
ABRUPTLY ENDED IN 1990 BY
A HEAVY FALL, WHICH BROKE
HIS RIGHT ARM IN TWO
PLACES, LEAVING IT
PERMANENTLY DAMAGED
EVEN AFTER PROLONGED
AND PAINFUL SURGERY.

T HE END OF Charles's polo career seems likely to please Diana, who finds it a boring spectator sport, and can resent its intrusion upon family weekends. These are anyway rare enough in a schedule as crammed with hardy perennials as the royal calendar. The Princess of Wales has had to learn to adapt to a series of fixed points in her year, over many of which she is given no choice: Christmas at Windsor, New Year and Easter at Sandringham, Balmoral in August. If she spends less than the Queen's statutory ten weeks at Balmoral, she is required to be there for annual events such as the family's visit to the Highland Games at Braemar and HMS *Britannia's* excursion to the Queen Mother's Castle of Mey.

T O CHARLES'S commitment to Klosters in March, she has managed to add a fortnight in Majorca each July with King Juan Carlos of Spain and his family (as well as her own Caribbean break with her mother and sisters). If Ascot in June can be a chore for a young woman indifferent to horses, it is at least a chance to shine sartorially, and the perk of a front-row seat at Wimbledon beckons soon after. Several times a year her attendance will be required at state banquets for visiting heads of state, adding to a host of annual royal 'musts' from the Queen Mother's birthday celebrations in August to the Armistice Day service at the Cenotaph in November.

I N THE MIDST of all this, Charles and Diana will also undertake two or three official foreign visits each year, extended tours halfway round the world, during which the strains of royal life are often at their most acute.

DIANA'S ANNUAL CARIBBEAN HOLIDAY IS A SPENCER FAMILY TRIP WITH HER MOTHER (LEFT) WHILE THEIR SKIING TRIPS TO KLOSTERS ARE OFTEN SHARED WITH THE DUKE AND DUCHESS OF YORK (ABOVE).

VII

FLYING
THE
FLAG

———— · ————

Sending the Prince and Princess of Wales abroad is a costly, complex and protocol-ridden business – a large-scale military operation with diplomatic overtones. On official visits the costs are borne by the taxpayer, as the couple are travelling as unofficial ambassadors for Britain. Private trips are naturally financed out of their private income from the Duchy of Cornwall (though they are always free to use the royal yacht, *Britannia*, or aircraft of the Queen's flight, both maintained out of the public purse). Either way, there are a thousand diplomatic and logistical niceties to negotiate before they can even contemplate leaving their native shore.

IN COMMONWEALTH countries, for instance, whether monarchies or republics, the Prince and Princess travel as members of the royal family; when making the arrangements, Buckingham Palace bureaucrats accustomed to getting their own way must heed the sensibilities of local hosts. Elsewhere they travel in official pursuit of the British government's foreign policy, and the Palace must make it clear that the usual diplomatic courtesies are the very least they expect.

THERE MUST, for example, be official receptions on both sides, hosted respectively by the British Ambassador and the head of state or his representative, at which the Prince and Princess will be the guests of honour. There must be a chance for the local British community to meet them. There must be visits to industry, especially any with British connections; there must be visits to the local armed forces (at which the Prince must wear the appropriate uniform); there must be private talks with the president, prime minister, foreign minister or their equivalents – mayors or other civic leaders when outside the capital city, the Pope if in Rome.

THERE MUST BE guards of honour for their inspection on arrival and departure, and at all appropriate points in between. The Prince's personal flag must fly from the cockpit of the plane on arrival, and alongside that of the host country on the car at the head of each

motorcade. A separate daily programme must be drawn up for the Princess, emphasizing the distaff side of things without becoming too frivolous. For either Prince or Princess, tree-plantings and plaque unveilings are tolerable, but should be kept to a minimum.

HOSPITALS AND specialists are alerted at points along their route; their medical records are sent out ahead of them. Menus and accommodations are inspected in advance; guest lists are screened; modes of address, seating plans, who enters which room in what order, who wears what decorations when – all requirements are painstakingly spelt out by the couple's representatives when, as in the United Kingdom, they travel the entire route in advance.

OFFICIAL VISITS will have been pencilled in at least a year ahead, after protracted negotiations between the host country and resident British diplomats. A month or two before the official departure date, the Prince of Wales's private secretary, press secretary and detective, along with one of the Princess's ladies-in-waiting, travel out to pre-plan the trip in the minutest detail.

THEY BASE themselves, wherever possible, at the British Embassy or High Commission, as it is British diplomats abroad who will bear the heaviest share of the considerable administrative burden. In consultation with host diplomats, the private secretary will vet the host country's proposed programme in the minutest detail. The detective will discuss security with his local counterparts; the press secretary will ensure that local journalists understand the nature of their prey – no spontaneous questions, no undue familiarity, no press conference and no political remarks – and that the travelling British press will have ample facilities to relay the good news (and pictures) back home.

ON TRIPS OF ten days or more, even before his marriage, as many as fifty items of luggage travelled out under the supervision of the Prince of Wales's baggage master. The author once found himself sharing the hold of an RAF Hercules with the Prince of Wales's luggage, travelling up the Amazon in advance of the smaller aircraft carrying the Prince and his staff. Half the aircraft's bulk was a wonderworld of pleasantly battered red trunks bearing the Prince's name and insignia; old-fashioned hat boxes marked 'straw' and 'top'; trunk upon trunk of military, naval and air-force uniforms – not all required by the schedule, but on hand just in case. Leather cases bearing polo sticks protruded through the netting holding the whole lot in place.

THIRTY SUITS AND uniforms are the bare minimum the Prince needs, though his valets can rarely persuade him to venture beyond a choice of six dark ones – which, to the chagrin of photographers, all look exactly the same. For the Princess, of course, these figures must

be doubled. The couple also take full sets of mourning clothes wherever they go, in case of a royal death back home; even a black-edged version of their crested notepaper is on hand to continue, in such an event, the flow of thank-you letters. Finally, there are crates of gifts: gold cuff-links bearing the Prince of Wales's three-feathered insignia, signed photographs in silver frames, graded by their quality and size to the rank of the recipient.

SINCE THE ADVENT of Diana, the amount of luggage on an extended royal trip comes to well over 3 tons, invariably requiring a separate aircraft all to itself. Some twenty staff will accompany the couple, from travelling hairdresser to the assistant private secretary's assistant. Even the Princess's lady-in-waiting merits her own dresser. Occasionally these ranks will be swelled by special advisers with local knowledge. The British Ambassador will greet them upon arrival, and the staff of the British Embassy or High Commission will be at their disposal throughout their visit. Wherever they may be in the world, the flow of red boxes to the Prince continues, and each day brings a Central Office of Information digest of British newspapers. Constant contact is maintained with Buckingham Palace.

BEFORE HIS marriage, the Prince would often make long-haul flights aboard scheduled aircraft, preferably the British carrier for the route, whose first-class sections would have been reserved for him and his staff. Nowadays air-force jets, sometimes sent by the host country, are required to cope with the vastly increased size of the party. On flights of a thousand miles or more, beds will be installed for the Prince and Princess's use. They will change out of their finery after the airport

IN SPAIN, A LATTER-DAY SIR WALTER RALEIGH SMOOTHS THE PRINCESS'S PATH.

farewells, and change back into it before the arrival ceremonies. RAF fighters will escort them through British airspace, and hand them over to the protection of the air force of each country they overfly. On shorter flights around Europe, the Prince will often take the controls of a BAC-111 of the Queen's Flight, which have at last replaced the antiquated, twin-engined Andovers of which he and his father were so fond.

IN THE PAST hundred years, Princes of Wales have forged their early reputations as much abroad as at home. In the 1870s and 1880s, the mid-period of his long decades of unemployment, the future King Edward VII went on protracted, swashbuckling tours of India, Egypt, Europe and the USA, occasionally travelling incognito, always taking a huge and costly retinue, invariably free to enjoy himself with even more abandon than at home. In like fashion, immediately after the First World War, the future Edward VIII embarked on tours through Canada and the United States, New Zealand and Australia, and later Africa; success after success was reported in the British newspapers, his ability to draw huge crowds anywhere in the world only serving to increase his popular glamour back home. The only Briton occasionally unimpressed was his father, King George V; when Edward was preceded home by such headlines as PRINCE GETS IN WITH THE MILKMAN, chronicling his nights on the town until 5.00 or 6.00 a.m., the King forbade any of his sons to visit America again.

PRINCESSES OF WALES have not had such fun. The first to hold her title in the jet age, Diana has already travelled far more of the world than all her predecessors combined. Charles, in the family tradition, had been several times around the globe before he even met her; he is, after all, heir to the most travelled monarch in history. Now the first decade of their marriage has seen Diana escort her husband to more than thirty countries, learning just how punishing royal schedules can be.

THE PRINCE AND Princess of Wales average three official overseas visits together per annum, at least one an extended voyage through a far-flung Commonwealth country. Charles makes many

more such visits alone, as increasingly will Diana; but outposts of what was once the British Empire naturally like to see them together. For three weeks or so they must pack an enormous number of suitcases, bid their children farewell, and gird themselves for an exhausting schedule in which even the few offstage moments afford little opportunity to relax.

IN THE DECADE since their marriage, Charles and Diana have made three official visits to Australia and New Zealand, two to

Canada and one each (as yet) to Japan, Fiji, Thailand, the Middle East (Oman, Qatar, Bahrain and Saudi Arabia), Italy, Austria, Portugal, Belgium, Spain, West Germany, France, Hungary, Nigeria, Cameroon, Indonesia, Hong Kong and the Philippines.

IN THAT PERIOD the Prince has also made thirty more overseas visits, to all five continents, on his own. Many of these were military missions, as Colonel-in-Chief of regiments stationed in West Germany, Norway, the Netherlands and Cyprus. As director of the

...WHILE PAPUA NEW GUINEA SEES THE PRINCE OF WALES LIVING UP TO HIS TRAVELLING MOTTO: 'THE THINGS I DO FOR ENGLAND!'

Commonwealth Development Corporation he has been to Tanzania, Zambia, Botswana, Swaziland, Malawi and Kenya; his presidency of the United World Colleges has taken him to the United States, Canada, Venezuela, Italy and Monaco. He has represented the Queen at the funeral of President Sadat in Egypt, independence celebrations in Brunei, and Second World War anniversaries in France. He has received an honorary degree at Harvard and taken the salute at the Queen's birthday parade in West Berlin. He has been to Toulouse for the launch of the Airbus, to Holland as patron of the William and Mary Tercentenary Trust, and to Elsinore in Denmark for Kenneth Branagh's *Hamlet* as patron of the Renaissance Theatre Trust.

DIANA'S FIRST SOLO mission abroad was to represent the Queen at the funeral of Princess Grace of Monaco, tragically killed in a motoring accident in 1982. At the time, it was a deliberate public gesture by the monarch to show her confidence in her new daughter-in-law. But Diana's first major overseas visit in her own right did not come until 1988, when she went to New York as patron of the Welsh National Opera and effortlessly took Manhattan by storm. Her political maturity was to have been tested in a solo visit to Pakistan in the autumn of 1990, but it was postponed after the collapse of the Benazir Bhutto government. A joint trip to Brazil later that year was also shelved because of the Prince's need for further surgery on his polo-damaged right arm.

DIANA, MORE THAN her husband, has had to learn that foreign travel does not always broaden royal horizons. Abroad, the kind of problems she encounters at home can be redoubled. On a recent visit to Hong Kong, for instance, the Princess was photographed in a revealing red bathing suit by a local paparazzo, who had climbed atop an adjacent skyscraper to gain a bird's-eye view of her supposedly private rooftop swimming-pool. 'The incident epitomizes the dilemma of being Diana,' wrote *The Sunday Times* that weekend. 'How is she ever – short of abandoning her blonde highlights, gaining a couple of stone and slobbering around in unprincess-like clothes – to be taken as anything more than an exquisitely coiffed airhead?'

DIANA'S STATUS AS the world's number one cover-girl, in other words, came at a price. As long as she remained a royal clothes-peg, consciously exerting a pin-up hold over magazine readers the world over, her public work would come a distant second in the public psyche. As yet, her loyal tribe of fans would be hard pressed to name the specific causes to which she has lent her name; they see pictures

BEFORE TACKLING AN ARABIAN FEAST, DIANA CANNOT RESIST FLIRTING WITH THE CAMERA.

of her out and about, even making speeches at dreary-looking functions, but they still take more notice of what she was wearing than where she was or what she was saying. The same, broadly speaking, holds true overseas, where the work the royals do is usually more difficult and exhausting than it looks.

F O R   T H E writers and photographers travelling the world with the Waleses – known to themselves as the privileged customers of 'Windsor Tours' – life is a lot easier than it is for the group leaders. Between engagements, for instance, the attendant press can relax on their bus at the back of the motor-

DIANA HOLDS THE HAND OF THE WIFE OF HUNGARY'S NEW PRESIDENT, AFTER SHE HAD MELTED INTO NERVOUS TEARS.

cade, while the Prince and Princess are required to make polite conversation to the local dignitary escorting them in car number one. Small talk, that most exhausting of royal burdens, must continue through every meal, every official banquet, while others around them have the chance to rest from the rigours of the day. There is the ordeal of eating unknown local food, often worrying-looking concoctions regarded as delicacies by hosts expecting a clean royal plate. Even alone in their private apartments, there will be a constant stream of visitors who have not otherwise been slotted into the schedule. Royalty may not have to worry about airline connections or lost baggage, but nor can they drown their sorrows in a few gin slings beside the hotel pool. Unlike the Windsor Tourists, who tend to have an extremely good time, Charles and Diana usually head back home in need of a good holiday.

I N   A   W O R L D where everything is supposed to be pre-ordained, the royals are often at their most vulnerable when coping with the unexpected. In May 1990, Diana had a chance to prove the smooth Sunday editorial writers wrong, bringing her own personal touch to the art of diplomacy, when she solved an unusual crisis of protocol with all the resource of a seasoned royal veteran. The couple's trip to Hungary was the first official royal visit to Eastern Europe since the descent of the Iron Curtain. At a time of rapid changes in the Communist landscape, they were greeted in Budapest by a caretaker president installed only that week. His wife, Zsuzsa Goncz, was so overcome by her unexpected role as hostess to royalty that upon being introduced to the Princess, whose feet had barely touched the airport tarmac, she burst into tears. Diana simply took her hostess by the hand, and continued to hold it throughout the proceedings. It was an act of diplomacy more natural, adept and self-confident than many trained Foreign Office grandees might have managed.

IN NIGERIA AND Indonesia she had already learnt how to squeeze maximum impact out of foreign visits by combining a cause close to her heart with a photo opportunity unavailable in Britain. Following the public response to her work for AIDS victims, she became the first royal to visit leper colonies – another deliberate use of her role to help dispel the illusions of public prejudice.

WHEREVER HE is in the world, Charles will tend to evangelize about projects close to his heart: architecture, urban regeneration, the United World Colleges, the need for the energies of restless and unemployed youth to be harnessed. Occasionally he can be portrayed

SHARING A JOKE WITH AUSTRALIAN MANHOOD DURING A SURFING COMPETITION NEAR SYDNEY.

as pulling off a trade deal – though he will really be rubber-stamping negotiations already concluded by businessmen or governments. The fact of his presence, however, can swing such deals Britain's way – sometimes entangling him in the kind of commercial exploitation the royal family must avoid.

IN AMERICA HE once agreed to cut a giant birthday cake, only to find its maker's name iced in the middle. Only in that country, as well, could the royals let themselves be cornered into dinners where excited locals turn out to have paid thousands of dollars to meet them. Such lapses are usually the result more of bad advice than bad policy, though tricks are sometimes played. Before his marriage, the foreign press would occasionally bribe nubile young maidens to leap out of the crowd and kiss him. If he was surfing at Bondi Beach, they might even be topless. Such are the occasional perils of being born to one of the world's great inheritances.

IN AN AGE when the Queen will permit her only son-in-law to accept commercial sponsorship – some discreet services to Daks clothes or Range-Rover cars helping to pay off the expense of farming Gatcombe – the royals are moving increasingly closer to a commercial arena of which they must beware. Tradition dictates that neither the monarch nor her heir, nor either of their spouses, can ever be seen to endorse a commercial product – though the curious system of royal warrants, by which shopkeepers and manufacturers can advertise that they supply goods to royalty, seems to come perilously close. The thick end of this particular wedge would be the sponsorship of monarchy as if it were a sporting event: today the BBC might televise the Courvoisier Princely Polo Challenge, tomorrow the Pimms Opening of Parliament.

AS ENDLESS ARAB DIGNITARIES QUEUE TO BE PHOTOGRAPHED WITH HER, DIANA HAS TROUBLE KEEPING A STRAIGHT FACE.

IN THE FRAUGHT commercial arena of Britain's import-export relations, the exploitation of the royal couple abroad is one occasional trap which eludes the advance reconnaissance of their staff. Other-wise, these trips generate a degree of goodwill on which it is hard to set a price; the Foreign Office is as appreciative of Charles's and Diana's hard work abroad as are the countries lucky enough to host them. It is not just a question of flying the flag, but of showing many and diverse foreign cultures – the majority of whom have long since dispensed with their own monarchies – that Britain's future head of state and his consort are an intelligent and well-informed couple, concerned about mutual problems and anxious to help. The United Kingdom could hope for few better globetrotting advertisements.

DIANA OUTSHINES EVEN
THESE COLOURFUL
UMBRELLAS AT A FACTORY IN
CHIANG MAI, THAILAND

THE
TRANSFORMATION
OF A
PRINCESS

——— · ———

A year or so after the royal wedding, a national newspaper photographer spotted a familiar car illegally parked on a double yellow line in London, right outside a fashionable Knightsbridge store. It was a black Ford Escort, with a silver mascot on its bonnet in the shape of Kermit the Frog.

ANY 'SNAPPER' worth his salt knew that the car belonged to Diana, Princess of Wales. So this one lay in wait. Sure enough, the Princess soon emerged from the shop, her trusty detective in tow. When she saw the photographer gleefully recording a royal infringement of the law, a cloud passed over Diana's brow. Then she called him over.

ON THE EDGE of tears, she told him just how embarrassing it was for her when such pictures appeared in mass circulation papers. It had happened a couple of times before. When she begged him not to publish them, this hardened veteran of countless such pleas for clemency was putty in her hands. He took the film out of his camera, and handed it over.

NATIONAL NEWSPAPER photographers are not noted for such behaviour. Their picture editors would not be at all pleased to hear of the voluntary surrender of so newsworthy a picture. The story just goes to show with what expertise this particular princess was already exercising an almost hypnotic charm over the most hard-bitten of her admirers.

ALMOST A DECADE on, such scenes are unlikely to be repeated. The blushfully winning ways of 'Shy Di', which earned her so much mileage in those early years, are long gone. She can still act winsome for the cameras; but the coy, slightly gawky teenager of those engagement photographs has grown into an elegant, self-assured Queen-in-waiting. The visual transformation has been extraordinary. But so has Diana's cunning in pulling it off. At the beginning of the decade, she had made half the world fall in love with her by remaining very much the girl-next-door who couldn't believe her luck: a

THE GIRL-NEXT-DOOR PRINCESS (BELOW) HAS TURNED INTO A SUPREMELY SELF-CONFIDENT FASHION PLATE (RIGHT).

princess in the you-too-can-be-a-princess mode, wearing off-the-peg clothes from familiar chain stores, wide-eyed at her translation to a world of pomp and privilege. By its end she had become the precise opposite: the Princess on a pedestal wearing designer clothes other girls her age could not afford, living in Walt Disney-style castles and palaces as if to the manner born.

THIS IS HOW the British like their princesses. They are required to be fantasy figures with an almost supernatural presence, leaving a trail of stardust in their wake. Diana's physical transformation is remarkably evident from the pictures on these pages; the gaucheness and puppy fat attending the end of her teens are now a distant memory, preserved for posterity in the iconography of her engagement and wedding. Only pictures such as these can trace her otherwise imperceptible progress up the mystical royal ladder into a dream princess, a visually flawless mirage of elegance – carrying a more potent symbolism than perhaps even she can understand.

RECENT HISTORY SUGGESTS that if Diana, Princess of Wales, did not exist, someone would have had to invent her. Though she has added a significant new dimension all her own, however, it is not insignificant that the history of the British royal family for the last 150 years has been that of a predominantly matriarchal society.

THE PERIOD BEGINS and ends with the two dominant monarchs of the era, Victoria and Elizabeth II. The central half-century of male monarchy consisted of three kings whose characters were shaped by their wives, and one who gave up his throne for a woman. Edward VII and George V married formidable foreign princesses who outlived them by many years, creating the figure of the venerable, elderly female personage now so familiar a part of the royal scenery. It was almost entirely thanks to his wife that the shy, stammering Duke of York, pitchforked on to the throne against his wishes, metamorphosed into the resolute King George VI, a symbol of hope and stability to a country ravaged by war. Now the present generation boasts an array of royal females, home grown and imported, who all take very different approaches to

the tricky and ill-defined art of being a princess. When Diana arrived on the scene in the early 1980s, she had a wide range of case-histories to study.

HER ROYAL BAPTISM was performed by the Queen Mother, a woman whose role Diana looks set to inherit one day, but whose early history could scarcely have been more different. Twice Lady Elizabeth Bowes-Lyon turned down proposals of marriage from Bertie, Duke of York, second son of King George V. She, like Diana, had grown up in an aristocratic family on the fringes of the royal circle; unlike Diana, however, she had seen enough of it not to desire membership. The stiff formality of the household run by the gruff King George V contrasted uncomfortably with the happy informality of her own; Lady Elizabeth didn't even want to be a king's daughter-in-law, or indeed sister-in-law, let alone Queen herself. But her fondness for Bertie and subsequent history between them forced her hand. Now, in her nineties, Queen Elizabeth has been a widow ten years longer than

she was a wife, and it is in that widowhood that she has invented a royal role which never before existed. Queen Alexandra and Queen Mary, the widows of Edward VII and George V, retreated into gloomy, Victoria-like seclusion after the deaths of their husbands, playing an active role in family affairs but none in matters of state. Persuaded by Winston Churchill that, at fifty-one, she was far too young to disappear into a lifetime of mourning, the Queen Mother has since become the nation's universal granny, embodying all the qualities

SIX FACES OF DIANA, IN A DECADE OF TRANSITION FROM SHY TEENAGER TO INTERNATIONAL COVER GIRL.

of warmth, dignity and integrity for which Britons look to their senior royals.

SHE MAY HAVE hesitated at Diana's brash start in the royal ranks, and especially at the cut of that notorious black dress, but the Queen Mother appreciated the importance of handing the torch to a new generation which would inevitably do things its way – and help to spread the royal workload. Princess Anne, by contrast, seemed to greet Diana's arrival with one of her periodic fits of the sulks. The only female of her generation to have to cope with the difficulties of being *born* a princess, rather than choosing to become one, Anne had not been blessed with film star good looks. 'No-one ever talks about what *I*'m wearing,' she sniffed of Diana's copious sartorial press coverage. But Anne had always put her own individuality ahead of anything artificial that might be expected of her; for most of her life, she had taken turns with her Aunt Margaret in being the royal black sheep needed by the press for pillorying on a slow day. In time they would both be relieved of that unenviable role by the latest new princess, Sarah Ferguson, Duchess of York.

DESPITE APPARENTLY stiff relations with Diana – she failed to attend Harry's christening, supposedly because she hadn't been asked to be a godparent – Anne continued to plough her own industrious furrow, and was soon giving the new arrivals an object-lesson in royal productivity. Through her tireless and assured work as president of the Save the Children Fund, she has rehabilitated her reputation beyond reproach in the public's eyes, and even entered the 1990s as a candidate for the Nobel Peace Prize. The Queen recognized as much in 1987, when she accorded her only daughter the title of Princess Royal, apparently to set her above and apart from the two *parvenu* princesses who at the time seemed more intent on having fun than buckling down to their royal duties.

THEY WERE SET a stern example by the 'lesser' royal princesses – Alexandra, the Duchesses of Kent and Gloucester – all of whom

SUPREMELY ELEGANT FOR AN ARTISTIC EVENING IN LONDON, AND SUITABLY SOMBRE (RIGHT) FOR A REMEMBRANCE SERVICE IN FRANCE.

earned their handsome Civil List incomes by undertaking scores of annual engagements with grace and aplomb, and espousing specific charities which benefit enormously from their patronage. The only exceptions were Prince and Princess Michael of Kent, curiously excluded from the Civil List, who endured long-running mockery from a press and public which did not understand their financial problems. Pre-Diana, Princess Michael was the foremost royal fashion trend-setter; she was also a colourful and outspoken character publicly satirized as 'more royal than the royals'. After a series of unfortunate episodes, from revelations about her father's Nazi past to her official opening of a motorway café, Princess Michael began to maintain a lower profile. In the fashion stakes, she had anyway long been upstaged by Diana.

ONE OF THE main advantages of women who marry into the royal family, rather than being born princesses, is that they have themselves shared the awe in which royalty is held. They are thus more readily able to put people at ease when on the receiving end of curtseyed bouquets, sycophantic speeches, tongue-tied handshakes or simply mindless adulation. It is a familiar and unnerving syndrome to those who meet Princess Margaret, for instance, that in private she can be so witty, warm and relaxed that they experience the rare *frisson* of being on an equal footing with a royal; one carelessly over-familiar remark, however, and the features will stiffen, the eyes harden, and there will follow a forceful reminder of who outranks whom. The same can be true, at times, of Princess Anne (and indeed Prince Charles). It is the legacy of a lifetime of deference – even at home, from fawning courtiers – which can at times lead even the most pleasant royals to remind outsiders of their place.

HAPPILY IMMUNE to any such trace of megalomania, Diana cleverly managed to retain many of her more endearing personal qualities while developing an increasingly cool and confident public style. In her first few years as a member of the royal family, the Princess of Wales was still very much her own woman. Many of those who have married British royalty have been content to submerge their personality in the corporate identity of the first family of the land. Not this princess. She was out to match her husband in the setting of precedents. Hitherto, for instance, royal protocol had been reluctant to risk the entire line of succession in one aeroplane; now Diana insisted that she, Charles and the children all flew to Balmoral together in the same aircraft, as would any other family. Remembering her mistake in taking William on tour to Australia, she was careful not to grow too militant in her ways; as an emollient to the Queen, for instance, she allowed herself to overcome her fear of horses, and underwent a little gentle coaching on a leading reign. Two years into her new life, her father was able to say of her: 'She is not shy any more. And she knows her own mind.' Earl Spencer felt confident enough to add that his grandchildren would 'grow up close to the Spencer side of the family, and be influenced by them as much as by the royals.'

AFTER A FEW early hiccups, the Queen became visibly delighted with Diana's progress. Having mastered the royal wave within days of her engagement, thanks to some expert coaching from the Queen Mother ('Imagine you're unscrewing one of those old-fashioned sweet jars'), the Princess's innate sense of fun brought a new dimension to the art of the royal one-liner. In 1983, in Australia, she found herself shaking hands with a one-armed man. 'I'll bet,' she said spontaneously, 'you have fun chasing the soap around the bath!' There was a tense moment, but no offence had been given. On the contrary, to laughter all round, any potential embarrassment had been cunningly defused. 'DIANA WILL KEEP me young,' said Charles, and there were those who thought she might well do the same, in the longer term, for the ancient and somewhat creaky institution of monarchy. Still in her early twenties, twelve years younger than her husband, Diana was soon keen to look more mature. She took expert advice from fashion consultants at *Vogue* magazine. Out went that famous mop of adolescent hair as she experimented with increasingly 'grown-up', at

THE ONCE BASHFUL PRINCESS NOW LOOKS HER PUBLIC SQUARE IN THE FACE.

times severe, styles. Usually she would retain the little personal adornments or variations which had been her early hallmark; in Australia, finding herself without the appropriate tiara, she simply wound a diamond choker around her head. These signs of her sense of fun, of an individuality which even the royal juggernaut could not smother, were the key to her continuingly unassailable popularity. Whatever rumours the tabloids threw at her, and however much they upset her personally, they did little to damage Diana's popular appeal.

THERE EMERGED, for instance, signs of resentment about the supposedly enormous amounts of money Diana spent on clothes. When one journalist, in 1983, calculated that it came to at least £1,500 a week, Diana buttonholed him at the earliest opportunity to challenge the figure. He explained his careful calculations, but was left none the wiser as to their accuracy. He might have been near the mark if all her clothes were purchased at retail prices.

THE ROYAL WARDROBE has in fact recently been valued at over £1 million. But Diana has sensibly made a point of being seen in various outfits more than once. In recent years it has been a debating point whether it is quite right for the royal females to wear clothes that could be recognized from previous outings. Diana sensed the obvious truth that the British people, themselves going through difficult financial times, would appreciate such conspicuous domestic economy. On a tour of Canada in 1983, it was calculated that of the thirty-five or so outfits Diana wore in three weeks, about twenty had been seen before.

IF HER INCREASINGLY stylish appearance was the outward symbol of Diana's rapid transformation, her natural and very feminine charm underscored it. Though no intellectual, she proved herself both savvy and street-wise, with an endearing line in self-deprecating humour. 'I'm as thick as a plank,' she told delighted office workers on a routine official visit, thus proving for sure that she wasn't. Nor was Diana unaware of the considerable sexual charms she exerted, even

WHEN THIS PRINCESS FORGETS HER TIARA, SHE CAN ALWAYS IMPROVISE WITH A CHOKER.

from a great distance, on her legion of admirers. She can scarcely be said to have flirted with foreign leaders, but countless photographs show how delighted they are simply to be in her presence. The same feminine wiles often proved useful, too, with her travelling retinue of reporters and photographers, whom she could beguile with a look, a smile, on special occasions a few words. There was no easier way of buying herself another tidal wave of positive publicity amid their colleagues' remorseless hunt for the negative. And it was not for merely personal reasons that a few of the full-time 'Di-watchers' confessed to falling a little bit in love with the Princess. She was the best story they had enjoyed for years, constantly keeping their by-lines on the front pages – adored by editors for boosting their circulations, and for providing a rare continuum of good news at a time when it was in very short supply.

BUT THE WATERSHED in the transformation of Diana was the arrival on the royal scene of her old friend Sarah Ferguson, who became Duchess of York on her marriage to Prince Andrew in July 1986. 'Fergie', too, was a new kind of princess: down-to-earth, rosy-cheeked, giggly and gossipy. A little too jolly-hockey-sticks for some tastes, the Duchess of York's public honeymoon was all too short-lived. Her husband had grown up with the nickname of 'Randy Andy', the wild card of the royal family, a figure accorded little public respect until he saw active service in the Falklands conflict of 1981. His bride seemed tailor-made, her brash sense of humour complementing his penchant for practical jokes and jolly japes of a variety uncomfortably associated with the idle rich. Prince Andrew had already made himself notorious by spraying press photographers with paint during a fund-raising visit to the 1984 Los Angeles Olympics; when both returned to California in 1987, their rumbustious, distinctly un-royal behaviour provoked widespread public dismay at home.

SARAH, ALAS, DID NOT share Diana's sylph-like statistics, nor her beguiling femininity. Apparently less concerned than the Princess of Wales about her figure, she nevertheless aspired to the same role in the fashion stakes, appearing in an array of dashing, even daring designs which she could not carry off with Diana's panache. Though continuing the flow of royal good news with the births of two daughters in rapid succession, she could never match Diana's unqualified popularity; and soon began to make matters worse for herself with a series of all too public misjudgements. She accepted free trips to exotic destinations, including the kind of hospitality from foreign governments of which royalty is supposed to beware. She wrote a children's book, which

would scarcely have sold in any quantity had she not married royalty, and reportedly pocketed most of the profits – rather than, as is the royal way, donating them to one of her public charities – in the face of a storm of public protest. Sarah, in short, neither looked nor behaved like a princess. Diana seemed positively regal by comparison.

F O R   A   W H I L E Diana's inexperience told, as her delight in the arrival of a new young friend in the royal circle led them to team up as a spirited royal double-act. Together they dressed up as policewomen to gatecrash Prince Andrew's stag party; at Ascot they were photographed, in all their expensive finery, prodding a courtier in the behind with their umbrellas. Diana's popularity wobbled. The monarchy's public standing was at stake. In the same way that it must be seen to rise above party politics, it must also transcend the class distinctions which still bedevil Britain. Andrew, Fergie and Diana, ably abetted by the young Prince Edward, were in grave danger of aligning the younger generation of royalty with the gilded youth of London's SW, not necessarily a heart-warming sight to the national rank-and-file. Diana swiftly withdrew to a safe distance.

NOW THE CONTRAST with the Duchess of York redounded more than ever to her advantage. Where Fergie seemed an over-excited, ungainly *arriviste*, Diana was every inch the prototype princess of whom Britain could be proud, and whom the rest of the world admired with envy. Though the two new princesses remained close friends, relieving each other's loneliness in the daunting world into which they had both married, Diana became very much the senior partner. 'If push comes to shove,' confided one courtier, 'the Princess of Wales is quite capable of reminding the Duchess of York who outranks whom.'

A TOUCH OF steel in the backbone was nothing amiss. In ten whirling years, Diana's life had of course changed utterly – but so, in the process, had she. The nation's memory of its first sight of her proved enduring: a teenage kindergarten teacher exuding innocence, so unworldly as to allow herself to be manoeuvred by photographers into standing against the sunlight, providing the world with the famous 'see-through' skirt shot. Now that tentative teenager had blossomed into a mature, self-assured woman of style and substance, as capable as any more experienced royal of carrying off in style both the grand occasion and the village visit. She had become a national treasure. The gauche little girl-next-door was now an ever more majestic Queen-in-waiting, who had single-handedly given the monarchy a new lease of life. Even more, perhaps, than her husband, she had come to symbolize the difficult transition ahead, from the second Elizabethan era to the unknowns of a new millennium.

DIANA'S NATURAL ELEGANCE WAS ENHANCED BY COMPARISONS WITH THE RATHER LESS SYLPH-LIKE 'FERGIE'.

IX

THE

TRANSFORMATION

OF A

PRINCE

The British constitution defines no role for the Prince of Wales. Its unwritten rules are eloquent as to what the monarch-in-waiting should *not* do, but stubbornly silent as to what he should. The history of the office, as a result, is not a particularly distinguished one.

PETTY RIVALRIES and jealousies have frequently set the heir to the throne at odds with the government of the day, even with the Crown in the shape of his own parent. The perks of the job, meanwhile, are considerable, offering a life of self-indulgent dalliance outside the maelstrom of political conspiracy. As Walter Bagehot put it: 'All the world and the glory of it, whatever is most attractive, whatever is most seductive, has always been offered to the Prince of Wales of the day, and always will be. It is not rational to expect the best virtue where temptation is applied in the most trying form at the frailest time of human life.'

THE TWENTY-FIRST English Prince of Wales in almost 700 years, the fortieth since the title was created in AD 844, Prince Charles Philip Arthur George must rank among the most intelligent and well-educated heirs to the throne in British history. Blessed with a strong sense of history, which he has also taken the trouble to study in depth, the young Charles was by disposition more earnest, reflective and conscientious than the majority of his predecessors. Early in life, he became determined to make his mark.

HE ENTERED his thirties, nevertheless, a lonely, confused bachelor still in search of a job and a wife. He has spent much of the ensuing decade adjusting to the discovery of both, while enduring mockery and backbiting as he espoused an array of minority causes not yet fashionable among the readers of the tabloid press. Yet he has recently embarked on his forties, and the second decade of his marriage, a popular and respected figure who has become a palpable force for good around the land over which he will one day reign. The first ten years of his marriage to Diana, have, in short, proved the most eventful and productive of Charles's life. It has been a remarkable transformation.

THE PRINCE'S mid-thirties were a period of great difficulty and doubt. Marriage to Diana had at last liberated Charles from the long and powerful shadow of both his parents, freeing him to pursue the philosophical and 'natural' interests close to his heart. Soon he had turned virtually vegetarian, and was exploring the benefits of holistic and other less conventional forms of medicine. He designed a wild-flower garden at Highgrove, about which he became obsessive, building at its heart a bower in which he took to relaxing and dealing with his paperwork. He began to practise organic farming on the

CONCERN FOR RACIAL MINORITIES HAS ALWAYS BEEN ONE OF THE PRINCE'S TOP PRIORITIES.

Duchy of Cornwall acreage adjacent to Highgrove, cut down on his public engagements and took to regular stints living the life of a Cornwall dairy farmer or a Highland crofter. The resultant headlines were staggering. 'A-LOON AGAIN', sniggered Rupert Murdoch's *Sun*. THE PRESS mockery was grossly unfair, but persistent enough to inspire public concern, much of it satirical. Was our future King becoming a bit of a crank? Among those who appeared to think so was his less romantic, ruthlessly down-to-earth father, who had never had much time for matters of the spirit, and now worried that married life was turning his eldest son soft.

ALL HIS LIFE Charles had been dogged by the shadow of Prince Philip, an athletic achiever at school and beyond, and a parent who had encouraged a particularly virulent strain of sibling rivalry among the royal children. It had led, in Charles's youth, to a rather hairy-chested approach to his leisure time which had earned him the tabloid nickname of the royal 'action man', parachuting, polo-playing, windsurfing, skiing. Having also inherited his parents' innate conservatism, he had hitherto tended to take physical risks at the expense of intellectual ones. The thoughtful, introspective, even at times eccentric Prince whom his future subjects now saw for the first time was the real one, his natural self – locked, perhaps, in the overdue embrace of the adolescence he had never really enjoyed, but able and anxious to pursue the inclinations of his inquiring mind.

THE ROYAL 'ACTION MAN' LOVED THE SURF AT BONDI BEACH.

HE EXPLORED the philosophy of Carl Jung, and travelled to African deserts with his mentor, Laurens van der Post, to study the primitive, unspoilt way of life of the Kalahari bushmen. Mortally prone to a sense of failure, Charles was trying to make sense of his own life as much as the eternal dilemmas of mankind. In his youth, he had confessed, he was capable of looking at himself in a mirror, dressed in scarlet uniform and bearskin before taking some salute, and wondering about the absurdity of what he saw. Royal life is so full of such flummery, and so remorselessly lacking in any routes of escape, that it requires an enormous leap of faith to take the whole business seriously. For a man with a pronounced sense of the absurd, his unchosen fate could at times seem a cruel and unusual punishment.

CHARLES WOULD NEVER share the daily chores and worries of most of his fellow men: from rising mortgage rates and school fees to changing nappies and washing cars. He would never get stuck in traffic jams, or fly on an airline which lost his luggage. His children were unlikely to trouble the school careers officer. His income was secure: the annual profits from the Duchy of Cornwall's vast land holdings, which free him from the need for a Civil List subsidy, bring in over £2 million a year. In this context, however, spiritual concerns can take on undue weight. Given time to explore them, for the first time in his life, Charles emerged as an embryo 'green', worrying about what he ate and drank, banning aerosol cans from the royal residences, persuading his mother to convert all the royal cars to unleaded petrol. From there it was but a short step towards fretting about the planet: the ozone layer, global warming, the destruction of the rainforests and all the other causes already fashionable among those dismissed by their opponents as 'the chattering classes'.

BRITAIN, MEANWHILE, had become an increasingly selfish society. The first Thatcher decade was creating an every-man-for-himself rush for wealth in which the devil was palpably taking the hindmost. Homelessness, urban blight and inner city decay were, to

Charles, the inevitable products of a post-industrial society, in which too little care was taken to regenerate once prosperous areas now fallen on hard times. Between them, the growing problems of Britain and the Commonwealth could surely provide this Prince of Wales with an opportunity to make constructive use of his office? Gradually, his speeches became peppered with references to the decay of the modern world, the loss of spiritual values, the injuries modern man was inflicting on himself and his planet. As yet half digested, and thus at times half-baked, the princely *pensées* earned him more tabloid mockery. But Charles became grimly determined to have the last laugh.

EVER PREPARED TO MAKE A FOOL OF HIMSELF, THE PRINCE OBLIGES PHOTOGRAPHERS WITH AN OLD AUSTRALIAN JOKE.

THERE WAS NO doubt about his conscientiousness, and his good intentions. What they desperately lacked was any focus. To the Prince, the irritating proof of this was the constant taunt, even from senior government ministers, that it was time he got himself 'a proper job'. He had founded the Prince's Trust while he was still in the Services; for more than a decade this and countless other personal initiatives had taken up the better part of his working life, involving him in long, hard hours of committee meetings, paperwork and speech writing, travelling all over the country to meet and encourage the beneficiaries of his various self-help schemes. To him, and to anyone who worked alongside him, this certainly amounted to a proper job – one he had painstakingly fashioned for himself out of the awkward, restrictive job description which came with his birth. To the British press and broadcasting media, however, Charles the glorified social worker was worthy but dull material, scarcely worth sending a reporter to cover

– unless, of course, the Prince was taking along his wife, in which case there would be a chance to lavish space on the new broad-brimmed hat, the changing Diana hairstyle, the latest fluctuations of the royal hemline. Inevitably, it would drown out whatever cause the Prince was trying to promote.

THESE DISTRACTIONS became so irritating that Charles soon stopped taking his wife along, in the hope that a few words of his speech might be noted in the quality papers. But the more fundamental difficulty remained. His work was far too piecemeal; his efforts were diffused around a bewildering array of trusts, initiatives and charities launched in his name, in a profusion which blurred his attempts to develop a central philosophy, and give his public work some cohesion. When a solution presented itself, its roots happened to lie in the very summer of his wedding.

THE HOT MIDSUMMER of 1981 was marked by two starkly contrasting events: the holiday atmosphere surrounding the royal wedding, and a rash of ugly riots and street violence the length and breadth of the country. High unemployment and inner-city decay, the twin hallmarks of the early Thatcher years, were dividing communities and igniting angry dissent. As the physical damage was counted in the tens of millions of pounds, the social cost was evaluated by a growing coalition of experts anxious to identify causes and seek solutions. By the time trouble erupted again four years later, on the Broadwater Farm estate in North London, the Prince of Wales had become deeply involved in efforts to improve the social conditions at the root of the problems. The summer of 1981 had blessed him not only with a bride, but with the sharp focus his public work so badly needed.

IT WOULD BE a few years yet before severe electoral losses in urban areas forced Margaret Thatcher to acknowledge the existence of any problem worth her government's attention around Britain's inner cities. In the meantime, a group of enlightened, somewhat maverick businessmen decided to take matters into their own hands.

Hard-line monetarist policies, they believed, were exacerbating industrial decline. Factory closures and mass unemployment were responsible for increasingly grim conditions around urban Britain – for levels of discontent, violence and crime among minority groups on the poverty line, especially young blacks, which might soon become irrecoverable.

THEIR SOLUTION WAS an innovative aid organization called Business in the Community (BiC). Its objective was to persuade major companies to donate sums of money, personnel or resources to be invested in community trusts, projects and local enterprise agencies designed to foster new business initiatives and thus new jobs. A catalyst for local action, inspiring partnership projects rather than managing them, BiC would act as an honest broker between the companies and the communities they served, creating mutual goodwill as much as mutual advantage.

BY 1984 BiC was looking to relaunch Project Fullemploy, an ailing scheme originally designed to promote new businesses and training programmes for unemployed black youth. The organization's chief executive, Stephen O'Brien, knowing that the Prince's Trust and its many offshoots had been especially active in this area, sought the Prince of Wales's support. Together they hosted a special conference in Windsor, an unlikely event at which captains of industry spent a weekend behind closed doors with leaders of the young black community, thrashing out mutual problems and seeking mutual solutions. Thanks largely to the tact and discretion with which the Prince chaired it, the Windsor Conference (as it became known) amounted to a major advance in race relations in modern industrial Britain.

WITH THE HELP of senior industrialists, O'Brien persuaded the Prince to take on the presidency of BiC, which began to co-ordinate its work with that of the Prince's Trust and its offshoots. The Prince's Youth Business Trust, for instance, was founded in 1986 'to educate, advise, and support young unemployed people with a view to setting up small businesses of their own'; to the small grants it awards – £1,000 maximum to individuals, £3,000 to groups – numerous healthy and growing companies all over the country now owe their existence. By liaising with BiC, these efforts could now be concentrated on specific areas – Calderdale in Yorkshire was an early example – where major regeneration projects were under way. Derelict factories were brought back to life; disused railways and stagnant canals were restored to full working order; old train sheds became craft centres and museums; countless jobs were created and entire communities given the chance of rebirth.

THERE WERE those, of course, who thought such philanthropy the job of government, and Charles occasionally courted political controversy as his inner-city 'crusade' began to mushroom. Although co-operation between the private and the public sector was a common creed to BiC and Downing Street, some of his speeches began to unsettle Tory backbenchers. By constantly drawing attention to inner-city problems, the Prince of Wales appeared to be venturing into the forbidden territory of party politics. After a meeting with the Prime Minister, a new charity he launched with the name of Inner City Aid – so called as a deliberate echo of the various movements inspired by Bob Geldof – was quietly shunted into

DRESSING UP IN OUTLANDISH UNIFORMS HAS ALWAYS PROVED A TEST FOR HIS STRONG SENSE OF THE ABSURD.

a siding. The Prince's public pronouncements were toned down, to avoid any charges of criticising government policy. It would be much more productive, even for a future head of state, to work alongside government than to court its disfavour. Besides, there were other less sensitive areas in which he could be as outspoken as he liked.

A PRINCE of Wales has no political power, but he has enormous influence. By appealing to the consciences of politicians he can act as a searchlight for social and economic problems, and a focus for efforts to solve them. King Edward VII, as Prince of Wales, though now better-remembered for his string of mistresses, prefigured his great-great-grandson by touring the slums of East London in disguise, as a member of a House of Lords inquiry into inadequate housing conditions. Prince Albert also anticipated Prince Philip, his successor as Prince Consort, by getting involved in the housing reform movements of his day. Charles would go one better, by meshing his concern for inner-city decay with his strong personal antipathy to much contemporary architecture. It was as if the pieces of a giant royal jigsaw – the many and disparate causes he had espoused – were suddenly falling into place.

SINCE 1984 THE Prince had been championing a movement known as 'community architecture', whose basic ideal is to offer those who have to live or work in a building as big a say as is practical in its design and construction. It was the kind of architecture practised by his cousin and friend, Prince Richard, Duke of Gloucester; Charles

THE CAMPAIGNING PRINCE HAS WON HIS SPURS WITH A DETERMINED INNER-CITY CRUSADE.

was further converted to the cause by a chance meeting at a Royal Academy dinner with another advocate, Jules Lubbock, architecture critic of the *New Statesman*. A few weeks later, the Prince was due to speak at a dinner celebrating the 150th anniversary of the Royal Institute of British Architects. He would use the occasion, he decided, to promote this worthy cause.

HE DID SO by singling out for public praise a number of practitioners of community architecture, including the then little-known Rod Hackney, who would shortly have his royal patron largely to thank for his propulsion into public prominence and the presidency of RIBA. This section of Charles's speech, however, was totally drowned out by his subsequent, savage attack on the rest of the profession, symbolized by the proposed extension to the National Gallery in Trafalgar Square, which he likened to 'a monstrous carbuncle on the face of a much-loved and elegant friend'.

THESE FEW WORDS were to become the most famous he had ever uttered. Charles had struck a public chord louder and more lasting than anything he had previously known. So popular were his broadsides against the architectural establishment – 'for far too long planners and architects have ignored the feelings and wishes of the mass of ordinary people in this country' – that he had soon become an *ex officio* arbiter of civic taste. Not merely was the National Gallery extension scrapped (and Charles appointed a Trustee of the Gallery, so as to approve its replacement); other long-term projects such as Peter Palumbo's dream of building a Mies van der Rohe design in the City of London fell victim to his displeasure.

CHARLES RELISHED his new-found power, oblivious to charges that it was not a Prince of Wales's job to pre-empt legal and statutory public planning procedures, let alone cause grievous commercial damage to the architectural practices he attacked by name. So powerful was his unofficial power of veto that nervous developers now took their plans to him for approval before proceeding. Three years later, with his equally celebrated pronouncement that British planners had done more damage to London than the Luftwaffe, the Prince undid years of work by a consortium of top developers and architects in the redesign of Paternoster Square. In the ensuing power struggle, his influence was sufficient to ensure that the area around St Paul's Cathedral will now be redesigned in accordance with his personal taste.

' I T   W O U L D   B E a pity if regeneration created eighteenth-century cities in the twenty-first century,' declared Prince Philip, in an obvious dig at his son which offered rare royal consolation for modernists. But Charles battled on regardless, championing classical designs and materials in a bestselling book and television documentary, even adding fake neo-classical detail to the exterior of Highgrove. To promote his book, the Victoria and Albert Museum devoted an exhibition to his ideas, built around ten royal commandments to architects. When his plans to build a 'model' village on Duchy of Cornwall land met with local opposition, then had to be abandoned, the Prince had an unwelcome personal taste of the complexities facing all planners and developers. But he has since had the confidence to found summer schools of architecture in Britain and Italy, designed to train a new generation of architects to obey his ten commandments.

T H E   S U C C E S S   O F his TV documentary, *A Vision of Britain*, encouraged him to make another, even more ambitious film on the earth's environmental problems. Filmed on location all over the world, it made less impact than the first, and attracted a good deal of dissent from experts. But it did continue to persuade the monarchist masses that this was a Prince who cared, who had thought long and hard about weighty global problems, and who intended to use his office for the common good. For the first time in his life, Charles was being taken seriously.

H O W E V E R ,   T H E   P R I N C E could still make surprisingly simple mistakes. When he decided to protest about contemporary standards of spoken and written English, it was unfortunate that his own speech was riddled with grammatical errors. His plans to form a nationwide legion of volunteers, supposedly to undertake social work where once they might have done national service, was inevitably ridiculed as 'Charlie's Army'. As his confidence grew, so did a trace of arrogance in his pronouncements: a strain of *de haut en bas* moralizing, in the hazardous royal tradition of 'we know better than you', which distanced him from the educated middle-classes and aroused the kind of public dissent from professionals to which princes are unaccustomed. CHARLES, IT emerged, was very good at dishing it out, but not so good at taking it. When the architectural establishment rounded on him, electing a new president who stood squarely in the enemy camp, he retreated into his shell. 'There is no need for me to do all this. But I can't just sit around and do nothing,' he blurted out to BBC

HRH THE PRINCE OF WALES
A
VISION
OF
BRITAIN
A PERSONAL VIEW OF ARCHITECTURE

HIS DISTASTE FOR MUCH RECENT BRITISH ARCHI-TECTURE LED TO A TV FILM AND BESTSELLING BOOK.

Radio's Brian Redhead. 'If they'd rather I did nothing, I'll go off somewhere else.' He needed, clearly, to develop a thicker skin, and to develop a fuller mastery of some of the subjects on which he felt free to pronounce. His famous stubbornness, which would turn a deaf ear to advisers urging caution, lost him a string of senior staff; two private secretaries, Edward Adeane and Sir John Riddell, resigned in quick succession when the Prince ignored the advice for which he supposedly paid them. Press secretaries, too, came and went in strikingly short order.

ALL OF WHICH mattered not a jot to the vast majority of his future subjects, who now saw Charles as a crusader prince, amibitiously anxious to protect Britain's cultural heritage and secure better working and living conditions for their children. Charles, too, was finally rid of the doubts which had haunted his first three decades. He had at last developed a personal vision which would brook no doubts or hesitations. Energized by a bold new self-confidence, he pre-empted critics and disarmed audiences with some gentle self-mockery at the beginning of every speech, on whatever subject, calling himself such names as 'a frightful reactionary imbecile' before anyone else did. Behind it all lay a personal decision of the greatest significance.

EVER PRONE TO self-pity, Charles had spent thirty of his forty years sharing the universal dismay that he would have to spend the majority of his life waiting in the wings for the job to which he was born. But in the last five years, especially through the response to his architectural outbursts, the Prince has realized how much more freedom of movement is available to a Prince of Wales than to a monarch. As King he will have to be much more circumspect; he would certainly not be able, for instance, to pre-empt public planning procedures and damage architects' careers by denouncing proposed civic buildings as 'monstrous carbuncles'.

THUS PRINCE CHARLES made a conscious decision to turn necessity to advantage, and to make his mark in history as a crusading Prince of Wales. It was a decision which made sense of his life, and offered a constructive use of the platform afforded him by the accident of his birth. He would relish the occasional controversy involved, in direct proportion to the influence he would savour even more. Having securely made his mark at home, and instituted organizations to put his ideas into practice, he would turn his eyes abroad, and spend his forties trying to make his mark as a figure on the international stage.

EARNESTLY REFLECTIVE BY NATURE, THE PRINCE HOPES TO USE HIS OFFICE TO HELP THOSE LESS FORTUNATE THAN HIMSELF.

ONE DAY, AFTER all, he would be King not merely of Britain, but of a dozen Commonwealth countries and dominions. By his mother's Golden Jubilee in 2002, when she will be seventy-five and he fifty-three, it will be vital that the British monarchy be regarded as a relevant, contemporary force for good in the modern world, rather than an antique, outmoded repository of hereditary wealth and privilege. The responsibility for this critical transition will largely be down to him. Public perceptions of Prince Charles and his older son will symbolize the monarchy's chances of survival into a new – and perhaps more sceptical – century.

THE OFFICIAL biographer of Lord Mountbatten and King Edward VIII, Philip Ziegler, observed in his book *Crown and People* that the British 'like their monarchs either old, wise and paternal, or young and hopeful'. A sixty-year-old King Charles III, Ziegler argued, would be neither. The logical conclusion was for the Queen to hand the Crown straight on to her grandson, Prince William: 'The Golden Jubilee of 2002 might be a suitable occasion.' Ziegler was gracious enough to concede that this might be something of a waste of the present Prince of Wales, requiring as it would his 'premature disappearance… the need for which he might consider inadequately proven.'

MANY MORE Britons, perhaps, would now agree with that sentiment than when it was first expressed in the late 1970s. The Prince's Trust has grown enormously since its involvement with

CHARLES CHOSE TO CELEBRATE HIS FORTIETH BIRTHDAY WITH BIRMINGHAM BENEFICIARIES OF THE PRINCE'S TRUST.

Business in the Community has tightened the focus on Charles's kaleidoscopic public work. Gradually, during his forties, it will seep into the public consciousness that Carl Jung, the United World Colleges, organic farming, homoeopathic medicine, community architecture and the regeneration of Britain's post-industrial inner-city landscape are all parts of a giant jigsaw which piece together as a cohesive world view. Between them they amount to a princely Bill of Human Rights, based on his belief in the innate qualities of the individual, and his or her right to live in decent conditions as part of a caring, prejudice-free community which functions smoothly and effectively.

IT IS A PERSONAL vision entirely befitting a future King. Charles's work towards achieving it, both in Britain and around the Commonwealth, is a crusade which (despite its few wobbles) does pride to the chequered history of the twenty-one English Princes of Wales. The next ten years will be a crucial test of his ability to put his ideas into practice, and to maintain their relevance to a rapidly changing world.

TOWARDS 2000:

THE

NEXT TEN

YEARS

Queen Elizabeth II has herself spoken of 'the uncertainty of human life', but the longevity of recent royal females seems to indicate that the Prince of Wales will be a grandfather in his sixties before he inherits the throne, the birthright for which he will have waited all his life.

FROM TIME TO time, meanwhile, there will inevitably be revivals of the great abdication debate. Should the Queen, as opinion polls increasingly suggest, retire early to give her son the chance to reign while at the height of his powers? It is an idea which has found growing favour with the public, during Charles's emergence as a crusader prince campaigning on issues with broad popular appeal. To many Britons, it seems a waste for so able an heir to wait well past his prime, to an age at which other Britons are drawing a state pension, before assuming the role to which he was born, and for which he has already spent years in training.

AS HUMAN BEINGS, both Queen and Prince would also favour some such premature transfer of office. After four decades on the throne, well past the normal retirement age for most British women, the Queen would be delighted to withdraw to the life of a country lady, devoting herself to horses and dogs rather than State papers and official engagements. Her son would naturally be pleased to have the chance of a long and productive reign, rather than his years on the throne being merely a brief butt-end to his life – as it was for the son of an equally long-lived mother, King Edward VIII.

AS CUSTODIANS of what they regard as a sacred trust, however, both agree that it can never happen. The idea was briefly discussed during Charles's teens, but has never been raised since. A consensus was reached, in consultation with politicians and churchmen of the day, that the Crown can never be allowed to become a pensionable job like any other, to be set aside at the age of sixty or sixty-five. The progression enshrined in the cry 'The King is dead; long live the King' is an essential part of the monarchy's mystique. Besides, the central

A RELAXED MOMENT AT BRAEMAR UNITES THREE ROYAL GENERATIONS.

characters involved never forget, unlike their subjects, that monarchy is as much a religious as a socio-political phenomenon. The Coronation is a sacred ceremony, involving vows and commitments which cannot lightly be broken.

FINALLY, AN abdication – even a 'happy' one, unlike that in 1936, the only abdication in British history – would set an uncomfortable precedent, as it already has in Holland. If the Queen were to hand over soon to Charles, would he not find himself obliged to hand over to his son William when he reaches sixty-five, probably a few years short of his Silver Jubilee? It would be inevitable.

HIS MOTHER AS MUCH AS
HIS QUEEN, ELIZABETH II
REMAINS THE MAINSTAY OF
HER SON'S LIFE.

So Charles and Diana cannot expect to move into Buckingham Palace until well into the twenty-first century. They will be such familiar figures, who will have waited so patiently for this moment, that their universal popularity will be assured. But beneath the regrettable accident of history which will have held Charles in the wings all his life lies a deeper dilemma that the couple must negotiate much sooner – primarily throughout this, the second decade of their marriage. Their contribution to the future of the British monarchy, whose survival will be very much in their hands, depends less on their own achievements than on their raising a son fit to be king. In the history of the next hundred years, it has to be said, King William V is likely to prove a much more lasting and significant figure than King Charles III.

This is a chastening truth to confront as eight-year-old William, like his father thirty-five years ago, begins his lonely life at a boarding preparatory school, where he must learn to hold his own amid a schoolboy world which pays scant heed to rank or titles. It will not be easy for him – as his father, the only previous heir to have gone to school with other children, can vividly testify. Charles has recalled that the more like-minded boys, the ones with whom friendship seemed most natural, tended to hang back, not wishing to be seen to court favour; those who thrust their way into the royal presence were, almost by definition, less *simpatico*. Shyness, the young Charles's problem, does not (by all accounts) seem to be William's. But competing on equal terms for athletic and academic success will never be easy for one singled out for exaggerated scrutiny by the accident of his birth. William's parents will have a vital role to play in providing him with the stability and support for which his father uniquely understands the need. They have made a good start with another royal innovation; rather than sending William to Charles's old prep school, Cheam, they have chosen another, Ludgrove in Berkshire, which allows the children to go home at weekends.

CHARLES AND DIANA may well, in fact, find their second decade together defined more by the progress of their children than by their own continuing aspirations and enthusiasms. The campaigning Prince will be keen to press on with the causes close to his heart; he is especially anxious in his forties to carve himself out a statesman-like role on the international stage as well as at home. Diana's routine and preoccupations seem likely to alter little, apart from the strong probability that she will have more children.

BY THE AGE Charles is now, his mother had been married more than twenty years, and monarch for sixteen. As Queen, she was already dealing with her fifth prime minister. Unlike Victoria, who denied her son any role in affairs of state, Elizabeth II was shrewd enough to initiate Charles into the executive machinery at an early age. She shared with him the secrets of the 'red boxes' of Cabinet papers, and in 1977 accorded him the status of Privy Councillor, thus enabling him to develop informal and confidential relationships with the senior politicians of the day. In time, without formally abdicating, it is likely that she will gradually encourage him to take over certain roles and duties which are not, constitutionally, the exclusive prerogative of the monarch. He might well, for instance, conduct the State Opening of Parliament – as would have been the case in 1988, during the Queen's absence abroad, had not an unusually heavy legislative programme altered the parliamentary timetable. Even more likely, he will represent her at the Commonwealth Prime Ministers' Conference, whose far-flung venues make this an increasingly arduous annual excursion.

POLITICAL COMPLICATIONS have thwarted his undisguised hopes of certain quasi-monarchical roles which would have amounted to on-the-job training – as Governor-General, for instance, of Australia, even of Hong Kong during its handover to the Chinese. (In either case, Britons would anyway have protested at losing him and Diana for a period of several years.) There are, however, many other

state duties, beyond such routine chores as state visits and investitures, where he can gradually take a more substantial role.

BUT HOW CAN HE provide such incentives for his own children before he himself inherits the throne? Were the Queen to live as long as her mother – which seems entirely likely, especially with her expert medical attention – William will himself be in his thirties before his father becomes King, and he himself inherits the title Prince of Wales. Again, as throughout Charles's upbringing, Elizabeth II will have to look back to the lessons of recent history.

EDWARD VII, VICTORIA'S son, was born heir to the throne and Prince of Wales, as which he spent a record sixty years – another royal record, perhaps a less welcome one, which Charles may well break. His oldest son, Eddy, Duke of Clarence, has been pretty much buried by royal history, largely out of embarrassment, as he led an undistinguished, dissipated youth, scandalous enough for theories to survive to this day that he was Jack the Ripper. His only chance of salvation, Victoria advised, was 'a good, sensible wife with some considerable character'. Eddy dutifully proposed to the paragon they found for him, Princess May of Teck, but a month later dropped dead at the age of twenty-seven. His younger brother George thus inherited both his bride – Princess May was eventually to become George V's Queen Mary – and the succession, for which he too declared himself woefully unprepared.

A KEEN STUDENT of his family history, Charles is also aware of the uneasy coincidence that both second sons born to monarchs in this century eventually became King. Close analysis of the case-histories of Eddy and George, and of Edward VIII and George VI, trace the problems of the weaker brethren to their upbringing at the hands of stern, distant or themselves confused parents. The psychological difficulties of growing up in direct line of succession to the world's premier throne cannot easily be exaggerated – as Charles also knows all too well.

HISTORY MAY JUDGE CHARLES AND DIANA BY THEIR SONS, WHO WILL STEWARD THE MONARCHY INTO A NEW MILLENNIUM.

IN THE SECOND decade of their marriage, it is crucial that Charles and Diana offer both their sons the security and warmth of a stable, affectionate home life, as well as the considerable parental support they will need to survive, in their unique positions, in the alien world of the British public school. Ten years from now, on his parents' twentieth wedding anniversary, Prince William will be retracing his father's steps to Oxbridge, with Prince Harry not far behind. Their adolescence, a period when their father was at his unhappiest, will be all but behind them; their characters will already have been substantially shaped; immediately ahead of them will lie, whatever their personal inclinations, a compulsory stint in the Services. As the royal wheel turns full circle, they will then spend their twenties reliving the same twin agonies so publicly endured by their father: finding the right bride, while carving themselves a role in an uncomfortably crowded royal landscape. Even a generation on, their proximity to the throne will deny them the freedom accorded to their uncle, Prince Edward, to double a light royal workload with a career as a theatrical impresario.

BY THEN, IT seems likely, their father's sternly traditional views will blend happily with the more innovative, down-to-earth approach of a mother well-versed in royal ways. In her own youth she delighted the nation by relaxing a few of the royal rules; perhaps the most signal public service Diana can perform may, in time, be to encourage her children to do the same. She will continue to breathe into the monarchy the fresh air which has so revived it in the public esteem over her first ten years; while Charles will continue to devote himself to the belief that a Prince of Wales can best spend his time preserving the national character and heritage of the country over which he will one day reign.

HISTORY, HOWEVER, may finally judge Charles and Diana less by their own characters and achievements than by those of their offspring – to whom it will fall to steward an ancient, if venerable institution into the unknown demands not merely of a new century, but of a new millennium.

**MIRROR IMAGE: PREP
SCHOOL HEADMASTERS
GREET TWO EIGHT-YEAR-OLD
PRINCES; CHARLES IN 1957
(LEFT) AND WILLIAM IN 1990
(BELOW).**

John Spencer, 1st Earl Spencer = Georgiana Poyntz
1734 - 1783   1737 - 1814

John Charles Spencer   Georgiana Eliz
3rd Earl Spencer   1799 - 1851
1782 - 1845

John Poyntz Spencer
5rd Earl Spencer
1835 - 1910

Albert Edwa
7th Earl Spe
1892 - 1975

Lady Anne Spencer = Captain Christopher Wake-Walker, RN
b. 1920   b. 1920

Three sons, two daughters

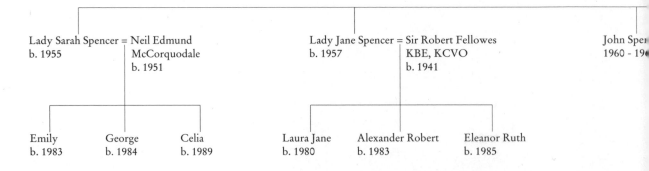

Lady Sarah Spencer = Neil Edmund   Lady Jane Spencer = Sir Robert Fellowes   John Sper
b. 1955   McCorquodale   b. 1957   KBE, KCVO   1960 - 19(
                       b. 1951   b. 1941

Emily   George   Celia   Laura Jane   Alexander Robert   Eleanor Ruth
b. 1983   b. 1984   b. 1989   b. 1980   b. 1983   b. 1985